# WASHINGTON

*The Story of Our Capital*

# A Prophecy

"The time will come when this wide waste of morass and thicket, open plain and wooded dell will resound with the busy hum of industry and be redolent with the glow of action and the thrill of life! The swamps along the Tiber, teeming as they do now with all varieties of animal and vegetable life, before the destructive march of men will gradually disappear, and Art will erect its palaces over the ruins of Nature." —From the records of the first Commissioners of Washington, January 5, 1795.

# WASHINGTON

## *The Story of Our Capital*

## Alberta Powell Graham

# THOMAS NELSON & SONS

### Edinburgh · New York · Toronto

Published in New York by Thomas Nelson & Sons
and simultaneously in Toronto, Canada
by Thomas Nelson & Sons (Canada) Limited.

*Photograph on jacket by courtesy of National Park Service.*

LIBRARY OF CONGRESS CATALOG CARD NUMBER: 53-9349

PRINTED IN THE UNITED STATES OF AMERICA
BY THE COLONIAL PRESS INC.

# Contents

CHAPTER

## *Planning the Capital City*

The thirteen British colonies in America, tiring of ever-increasing taxes and unjust tyranny, finally broke with England. They established a form of self-government.

The governing body, the First Continental Congress, assembled in 1774. It met in Philadelphia because that was then the largest city in the colonies, and was situated midway between the North and the South. The business of making a government, however, was interrupted by the Revolutionary War. The King of England, George III—unwilling to let these valuable colonies have their independence—sent his armies overseas to subdue the rebels. Then the Congress had to move its headquarters—not once, but many times—in order to keep out of the way of the invading British troops.

Our Continental Congress was forced to meet in eight different cities and towns. Congress had to gather up its papers and move in and out of Philadelphia four times, Princeton three times. It also met in New York City, Baltimore, Annapolis, Trenton, and York, and it even spent one day in the little Pennsylvania Dutch village of Lan-

7

caster. The war against England was finally won, and, in spite of interruptions, the members of this Congress continued to work out laws and plans for the new country.

But by 1786 these men were convinced that the Continental Congress was not a strong enough governing body to do all that had to be done. They met at Annapolis and issued a call for a Federal Convention. This Convention of 55 men met in Philadelphia and sat all through the hot, malarial summer of 1787. By the end of the summer—on September 17th, the day we still celebrate as Constitution Day—the work was done, and the Convention submitted the completed Constitution to the 13 states for ratification. It took more than a year for nine of the states to ratify the new organ of government. But finally, in 1788, elections could be held.

After General George Washington had led the American Army to victory in the Revolutionary War, he had become the popular hero of the country, and the people unanimously elected him President of the 13 states. John Adams was chosen as Vice-President and a Congress, of senators and representatives, was elected. In April 1789, the new Congress met, and General Washington was inaugurated as the first President. The meeting and the inauguration took place in New York City. It was a new Government, with a new idea behind it—the idea of a national power strong enough to accomplish those things on a national scale for which the people had fought and won a great war of independence.

The next business of the new nation was the establishment of a permanent place where the President and Congress could meet to make laws and attend to the government of the country. This place must be national, easily accessible, and fixed. And then the trouble began. The northern states wanted the capital within their boundaries, while the southern states were firmly determined that it should be a southern city. Different locations were suggested and hotly debated. One congressman even proposed that a large hall be built on a wheeled platform for the meetings of Congress, with a statue of Washington mounted on another platform, so that the capital could be moved from place to place. Money, land, and buildings were offered by 24 cities and towns to induce Congress to move in with one of them. But all of those tempting proposals were rejected and Congress agreed with the President that an entirely new city should be built for the home of the national government.

The lawmakers decided that the "Federal City," as the President called it, must be near the center of the United States, neither too far north nor too far south. At that time, although it is hard to believe today, Georgetown was considered the geographical center of the United States. The capital must not be too near the coast because of the danger of an enemy attack from the sea. It should be on a navigable stream, however, for at that time transportation was mainly by water. Journeys north and south were made almost entirely that way; and as the ships were all sailing vessels, dependent on the wind, their progress was slow and uncertain. Travel on land was also exceedingly difficult. There were few highways, and, of course, no railways. Most of the roads were simply wide paths cut through the forest, and many times snow and mud made them impassable. There was much heated talk over the proper location of the Federal City, talk that seemed to lead nowhere.

The question of the payment of the Revolutionary War debts was also being hotly contested at that time. As the Federal Government had been the result of the war, the North protested that the Government was responsible for the war debts. But the South, having had fewer states in the struggle, argued that each state involved should pay its own share. This led to many fiercely fought arguments.

Alexander Hamilton, the Secretary of the Treasury, was not interested in the location of the capital, but he did want the Government to pay the war debts. Thomas Jefferson, the Secretary of State, was more concerned with the site of the Federal City. He wanted it to be somewhere near his Virginia home. So Jefferson and Hamilton made a bargain—a bit of "log-rolling," still carried on today. Jefferson gave a dinner party. The leaders of both sides of the two questions were invited. Jefferson promised to get his followers to vote for the governmental payment of the war debts, if Hamilton would persuade his faction to vote for the location of the Federal City on the Potomac River. It was a grand dinner, with many choice foods and rare wines. By the end of the meal all the guests were in perfect agreement.

The bitter discussion as to which part of the country was most suitable finally ended. Congress voted to establish the capital city in an area 10 miles square on the north side of the Potomac River, somewhere between Alexandria and Georgetown. The exact location was left for the President to choose. Congress then moved from New York to Philadelphia where the members voted to remain for ten years, at the end of which time it was believed that the permanent capital on the Potomac River would be ready.

The territory selected was all familiar ground to George Washington, for his home at Mount Vernon was only 11 miles down the river from Alexandria. He had hunted in the woods when a boy; he had surveyed many of the fields, and as a young soldier, he had ridden through the region with the British commander, General Braddock. Sixty-four of those 100 square miles were in Maryland and the remaining 36 were in Virginia. Alexandria and Georgetown were both in this area. At that time Georgetown was fast becoming a busy market place, while Alexandria, then more than 50 years old, was a thriving tobacco-shipping port.

Of course this site did not please everybody. Much of the land near the Potomac River was low and swampy. People in Boston, New York, and Philadelphia laughed at the thought of building a capital city in a mudhole. Many declared that, for the first time, George Washington had shown poor judgment. Others continued to demand that the seat of government be located in an established city.

Nevertheless, the President went ahead with his plans for the Federal City on the Potomac. He appointed three commissioners: Daniel Carroll and Thomas Johnson, both from Maryland, and David Stuart of Virginia. Washington held many conferences with Thomas Jefferson, his Secretary of State. They realized that this national capital must be planned carefully and built quickly.

Jefferson drew a crude sketch of what he thought the city should be, but he fully agreed with Washington in believing that the capital must be designed by an expert. The designer must be skilled in landscaping as well as architecture, and he must be acquainted with the most beautiful cities of Europe. At that early period, America had no outstanding architects and no large cities to furnish inspiration for such an undertaking. But fortunately, just at that time, Washington received a letter from a young French officer, Major Pierre Charles L'Enfant, who asked for the privilege of designing the capital of the new republic.

"No nation," he wrote, "ever before had the opportunity offered them of deliberately deciding upon the spot where their Capital City should be fixed, or of considering every necessary consideration in the choice of situation; and although the means now within the power of the country are not such as to pursue the design to any great extent, it will be obvious that the plan should be drawn on such a scale as to leave room for that aggrandizement and embellishment which the increase of the wealth of the Nation will permit it to pursue to any period, however remote."

Washington and Jefferson were delighted. This writer seemed to share their ideas. They investigated and learned that Major L'Enfant was a young soldier who had come from Paris at his own expense to join the Continental Army in the Revolutionary War. Having been trained as a military engineer, L'Enfant had shown great skill in designing fortifications. He had been wounded in battle and taken prisoner. At the end of the war, L'Enfant had remained in America and was becoming well known as an architect and designer. While remodeling Federal Hall in New York City, he had heard of the new capital city and made up his mind to have a part in its planning.

Pierre Charles L'Enfant, the son of a famous French artist, was born in Paris, August 2, 1754. He inherited his father's talent and was educated in the arts. Young L'Enfant had traveled widely and was familiar with European capitals and cities. Washington and Jefferson decided he was competent and at once engaged him to design the nation's capital.

On looking over the area, L'Enfant preferred the picturesque country near the Great Falls of the Potomac. But President Washington and Thomas Jefferson thought that the capital might also have a future in commerce and shipping. Therefore they insisted it should be located near the ports of Alexandria and Georgetown.

Washington attended to the business of buying the land. There were 19 landowners in the area, most of whom were farmers whose chief crop was tobacco. The

Government agreed to pay 25 pounds sterling—or $66.66⅔—per acre for all land which was to be used for public buildings and grounds. The owners were to make no charge for the land used in highways, streets, or parks. The remaining acres were to be divided into lots which were to be shared equally by the owners and the Government. It proved to be a satisfactory settlement for sellers and purchasers, and Jefferson declared that Washington's management of the business was "truly noble."

Major L'Enfant had no trouble in choosing the location for the congressional house or capitol building. He gazed up the long slope from the marshy banks of the Potomac River to the top of the hill more than two miles away, and pronounced it perfect. This was Jenkin's Hill, the highest point in the nearby area, 88 feet above the level of the Potomac. L'Enfant declared that it was a "pedestal awaiting a monument," and it was there he marked the spot for the "Capitol," which was the name he gave to the congressional building.

The young major designed a grand avenue, to run diagonally across the city from the southeast to the northwest, and named it Pennsylvania for the state which was the home of the first capital. On this avenue, a mile and one half northwest of the Capitol, he reserved a plot of 80 acres, then mostly swamp, for the site of the President's Palace. Congress, thinking of the expense, suggested that the President have his living quarters in the Capitol building. But George Washington insisted that the President should live at least one and one-fourth miles from the Hall of Congress.

L'Enfant planned the Mall, a broad, grassy parkway extending west from the Capitol grounds to the banks of the Potomac. He meant to use Tiber Creek, which flowed across the area, turning west at the base of Capitol Hill, and continuing to the Potomac, in a series of cascades in the center of this space. Rose gardens were to border the sides of the Mall, also serving to beautify the lawns of the foreign embassies which L'Enfant planned to build adjoining this long park. Midway down the Mall, he fixed the location of an equestrian statue to be erected in honor of President Washington.

The streets of the new city were to be 100 feet, and the avenues 160 feet in width. In the many small, circular parks at the intersections of the streets and avenues, L'Enfant planned to mount cannon which could be faced in different directions for the defense of the city.

Washington and Jefferson agreed with L'Enfant's ideas and the three men held frequent conferences to discuss the progress of the plans. They met at Suter's Inn, a small yellow house at 3049 M St., Northwest. This house, still standing and in good repair, was purchased by the Government in 1952 to be kept as a museum.

It was decided that the capital, which had often been spoken of as Washington City, should be called "The City of Washington," in honor of the President. Washington modestly objected to this use of his name; in fact, he spoke of the town as "The Federal City" to the day of his death. The area within the 10 mile square was named "The Territory of Columbia."

L'Enfant divided the city into four sections: Northwest, Northeast, Southwest, and Southeast, with the Capitol as the center. The streets running east and west were named for the letters of the alphabet, omitting the letter "J" because it looks so much like the letter "I." The streets leading north and south were named with numbers: First Street Northwest, Northeast, Southwest, or Southeast according to the direction from the Capitol. The avenues, radiating from the Capitol like the spokes of a wheel, were named for the states toward which they pointed.

That is the way the streets are today, more than one hundred and sixty years later.

Early in August 1791, Major L'Enfant sent his first design of the capital city to President Washington. He had indeed allowed for the "future growth of the Nation." His plans were made for a city of 800,000 people, the population of Paris at that time. L'Enfant didn't dream that Washington would ever outstrip Paris in population, but today our rapidly growing capital contains over a million people.

This was the first time that a complete design for the capital of any country had been made. In no other nation had the capital city been planned in its entirety, with parks, public buildings, streets, and even the spots selected for churches, colleges, monuments, and markets. All this was done before the forests had been cleared from the land, or the streams and marshes drained from its surface.

How the people laughed at the "crazy Frenchman's highfalutin ideas"! And there was ample cause for their amusement. It was unreasonable to expect that people traveling along muddy paths and Indian trails through the deep woods could visualize the broad, tree-lined streets, marble palaces, and monuments which L'Enfant had planned.

L'Enfant could not work easily with other men. Although he had great ability as an architect, he did not get along well with people, and he would not let anything stand in the way of his plans. At one time L'Enfant ordered a new residence removed because it interfered slightly with the view down an avenue. When the owner, a member of the wealthy Carroll family, refused, L'Enfant sent his workmen to tear it down in the night.

Money was badly needed to pay for labor and material

in the building of the new city, and the commissioners had arranged to hold an auction sale of building lots in an effort to raise funds. They asked L'Enfant to allow them to publish his plan of the city, in order to interest people in the sale. But he indignantly refused to let them have the design, declaring that it was just a scheme of grafters and speculators who were trying to get possession of the choice lots. The commissioners, angered by L'Enfant's lack of co-operation, begged Washington to dismiss him, but the President was unwilling to let him go with his work unfinished. However, when L'Enfant began work on the foundations of the Capitol without consulting the commissioners, or even mentioning it to anyone in authority, Washington regretfully discharged the man who planned this beautiful city.

CHAPTER

 2

## The Capitol

With L'Enfant's dismissal, work on the Capitol building ceased. No one knew just what to do. The commissioners had in their possession L'Enfant's plans for the city but none for the buildings could be found. David Ellicott, who had been L'Enfant's assistant, was appointed to lay out the streets and parks.

Offering a prize of $500 or a gold medal for each contest, the commissioners then advertised for plans for the President's Palace and the Capitol building. James Hoban's design for the President's Palace was accepted and work was immediately begun. The cornerstone of this, the first government building in the new city, was laid October 13, 1792, three hundred years and one day after Columbus had caught his first glimpse of the new world.

The prize-winning plan for the Capitol came from William Thornton, a native of the West Indies. Dr. Thornton was an inventor, an artist, an amateur architect, and a graduate in medicine who had been educated in Scotland and had traveled extensively; he knew the

17

necessary requirements of such a building. Thornton came to the United States, established his residence in Washington, and personally took charge of the first work on the Capitol.

On September 18, 1793, the President laid the Capitol's cornerstone. People came from all the country around—more than 1,500 of them—to the first public celebration in the new city. It was also the occasion of the first of the thousands of parades that Washington has seen.

The procession formed in the President's Park, now Lafayette Square. Two bands and two companies of artillery, followed by officials, workmen, and citizens, proudly marched to the Mall. Here they were forced to lay aside their dignity, and slowly, one at a time, walk on a footbridge made of logs, across Tiber Creek. Still in single file, they hurried along the narrow path—there was no street—to the top of Jenkin's Hill.

After a program of prayers, songs, and speeches, President Washington laid the cornerstone. With a silver trowel, which has been used many times since, he pressed the mortar in place around the stone. Then the crowd gathered around the tables nearby where a barbecued ox and a picnic dinner were served free to all.

When Congress adjourned on June 11, 1800, Philadelphia was no longer the capital of the United States. President John Adams journeyed down to Washington and found the north wing of the Capitol, which was the part first built, ready for occupancy. Records, files, and all of the governmental papers were shipped from Philadelphia by water. The President, his Cabinet, Congress, and secretaries and clerks—136 people in all—traveling overland, arrived in October.

On Saturday, November 22, 1800, the Congress of the United States convened for the first time in Washington at a joint meeting in the Senate Chamber of the Capitol.

President Adams made a speech in which he said: ". . . It would be unbecoming the representatives of this nation to assemble for the first time in this solemn temple, without looking up to the Supreme Ruler of the Universe and imploring His blessing."

Every head was bowed as the President prayed: "May this territory be the residence of virtue and happiness! In this city may that piety and virtue, that wisdom and magnanimity, that constance and self-government which adorned the great character whose name it bears, be forever held in veneration! Here, and throughout our country, may simple manners, pure morals, and true religion flourish!" This custom of opening the session with a prayer has been followed to this day, both in the Senate and the House of Representatives.

One hundred feet south of the Senate Chamber the foundation of the opposite wing was laid. The open stretch between the buildings was used as a roadway or a short cut down the hill to the town. Also in this vacant space were two deep wells which furnished the neighborhood with its water supply. When the south wing was finished, a wooden arcade joined it to the north section, and the representatives moved into their new quarters in 1807.

Major L'Enfant wandered about watching the progress of the new buildings. He was a pathetic figure, tall and thin, wearing a long, shabby coat and a high-crowned hat. He always carried a large roll of papers under his arm, supposedly his claims against the Government. In his right hand he held a hickory cane with a large silver head. He talked to no one, but prowled around alone, followed by his faithful dog.

L'Enfant had no contract with the Government and he had been paid only the small sum of $600, for his expenses. Terribly hurt and offended when dismissed from his work on the capital city, he sued the Government for a huge amount but he received nothing. Washington offered him a building lot near the site of the President's Palace and $2500, but L'Enfant would not accept them. Appointed to a teaching position at West Point, he refused that also. Then Washington put him in charge of the construction work at Fort Washington. His ideas were fine, but again, through his inability to get along with people, he lost that job.

Mr. William Dudley Digges, a relative of the Carrolls, then came to L'Enfant's rescue. He invited the Major to visit him and plan an elaborate garden on his estate near Silver Spring, Maryland. And there, the gifted L'Enfant, poverty-stricken and pitiable, lived on charity throughout his remaining years.

In 1812 came another war with the British which brought disaster to the new capital. By 1814 the British fleet had been in control of Chesapeake Bay for more than a year and a half. Through all that time Baltimore and Washington were in constant danger of attack. Although President Madison and his Cabinet had been warned repeatedly of the probable invasion of the capital, they made no move toward its defense. Secretary of War Armstrong pooh-poohed the idea of invasion which, he said, could never happen.

But it did happen. Four thousand trained British troops under General Ross landed at Benedict, Maryland, on August 19, 1814 and prepared to march to Washington, 40 miles away. General Winder, with a small body of soldiers and the militia called from nearby states, met the enemy at Bladensburg. The President and the Cabinet were in the front lines of the Army. But when they saw the small force mustered for the protection of the capital, they took to their heels and hid in the Virginia woods. President Madison sent his groom with a note to his wife,

Dolly, who was at the President's Palace awaiting her husband's return, urging her to be ready to leave at once.
Daniel Carroll also came from the battle at Bladensburg
with a message for Mrs. Madison to leave the city immediately. Dolly Madison was busily packing the precious
state papers and the silver into trunks and boxes. Mr. Carroll was ready to help the first lady into her carriage when
she dashed back into the Mansion. "The enemy must not
take possession of General Washington's portrait!" she
cried. The brave lady stood by while her servants broke
the frame, and removed from the wall the large painting
of the first President; she then gave it to friends who carried it to a safe hiding place. Then the courageous Mrs.
Madison paused once more, to break the glass case containing the copy of the Declaration of Independence and
save that valuable document from capture, before she
drove away to Georgetown.

Winder's inexperienced soldiers were easily defeated
and the British forces invaded the capital city on August
24th. They burned the Capitol, the Treasury, the State
and Navy Building, and the White House. They prepared
to set fire to the Patent Office; but it was defended by its
director, Dr. William Thornton, the architect of the Capitol, who was as brave as he was talented. He met the in-
vaders at the entrance of the building and defied them.
"Are you English, or Goths and Vandals?" he shouted.
"This is the Patent Office, the depository of the ingenuity
of the American Nation in which the whole civilized
world is interested. Would you destroy it? If so, fire away,
and let the charge pass through my body!" Awed by
Thornton's words and valor, the attackers moved on, leaving the building unharmed. The British raid on Washington was stopped by a violent storm, a veritable tornado.
Wind, lightning, and a beating rain drove the British
back to their camps and extinguished the fires in the

ruined city. Many declared this storm to be an act of God.

The work of rebuilding the Capitol was begun without delay. The wooden arcade was replaced by a large central rotunda which was topped with a copper-covered, wooden dome. The restoration was completed in 1827.

The country grew, the number of states increased, more congressmen were sent to Washington, and the Capitol was too small before it was 50 years old. In 1851, President Millard Fillmore laid the cornerstone for new north and south wings adjoining the old ones. The new wings were ready for occupancy in 1857, but more time was needed to finish the dome.

This dome, the crowning feature of the Capitol, ranks as one of the six great domes of the world. It consists of two huge, cast iron shells, one inside the other, which contract and expand as the temperature changes. The base of the massive Capitol dome is surrounded by 36 columns, representing the number of states in the Union at that time. The dome is capped by a "lantern" which is a circle of windows supported by 13 columns, corresponding to the number of original states, and on the very summit of the dome, 300 feet above the Plaza, stands the statue of Freedom. This inspiring bronze figure, 19 feet in height, was made by Thomas Crawford, an American, in his studio in Rome. The vessel in which the original plaster model was shipped to America sprang a leak at Gibraltar, foundered at Bermuda, and was more than a year en route.

Jefferson Davis, at that time Secretary of War, objected to the cap on the statue, a French liberty cap encircled with stars. He said it was like the caps worn by the freed slaves and, therefore, not fitting for Freedom's head. The liberty cap was then changed for a helmet adorned with eagle's feathers, not nearly so attractive as the original headgear.

During the Civil War, President Lincoln insisted that the work on the Capitol dome be continued. He felt that the Capitol was a symbol of the Union, and that even a war between the states should not prevent its completion. So, while the battles raged between the North and South, workmen on the high scaffolding around the dome labored to complete the home of the Government.

On December 2, 1863, to the noisy accompaniment of a national salute of 35 guns and wild cheers from the crowds overrunning the Capitol Plaza, the statue of Freedom was raised to her place atop the dome. This was the crowning touch. After 70 years in the making, the nation's Capitol was finished.

The stately dome is beautiful by day, and at night, with the figure of Freedom silhouetted against the sky, it is an unforgettable picture.

Many people wonder why the statue of Freedom faces east. The fact is that Major L'Enfant planned the city to develop east of the Capitol. But the real estate speculators and the landowners in that section asked such unreasonable prices that no one would buy the lots and, instead, the city was built northwest of the Capitol. So Freedom's back is turned on the beautiful view down the Mall and she faces the rising sun.

Few, if any capitols in the world surpass in beauty that of the United States. The location is superb. Against a background of tree-clad hills the majestic building stands at the top of a gentle slope rising above the Potomac River. With its beauty and size, the Capitol dominates the landscape; in fact, since Thomas Jefferson's time there has been a general agreement that no buildings, public or private, in downtown Washington shall reach higher into the sky than the Capitol dome.

There are 58 acres in the grounds immediately surrounding the Capitol, terraced and beautifully land-scaped with hundreds of trees and shrubs. Many of the trees have been brought from foreign lands, but they all seem to thrive in the mild climate of the Washington area.

The Capitol has two fronts, one facing west and one east. The west front overlooks the Mall and Pennsylvania Avenue but, because there are many steps, most people avoid the long walk up the terraced lawn and use the more familiar east front.

The east front opens on the Plaza. And here one can see where Maryland, Pennsylvania, Delaware, and New Jersey Avenues all join to make the hub at the Capitol. This Plaza, which includes the open square and the park beyond, plays an important part in the life of the capital city. Here the vast crowds gather to see the inauguration of the Presidents; here the cheering throngs welcome home the conquering heroes from the battle fronts; and here on summer evenings old and young assemble to listen to the band concerts.

The main stairway of the central portico of the Capitol leads to immense bronze doors, as fine as any in the world. The carvings on the doors tell the story of Columbus' discovery of America. These doors open into the rotunda, the great reception hall of the nation. Here, under the dome, many famous men and women have been welcomed; and here also, the bodies of many of our great men have lain in solemn state.

But this noble room was not always reserved for national affairs. In its early years, anyone who wished to could occupy it. Bazaars, benefits, teas, panoramas of Paris and other cities, and exhibits of manufactured products were held there. The rotunda became a regular market place where anything from a mousetrap to a saddle, a stewpan to a piano might be bought and sold. However, in 1828 Congress put a stop to such uses, or rather, misuses, of the Capitol.

The rotunda is richly decorated with paintings and sculpture. Just inside the doors stands a statue of George Washington who seems to be looking over the marvelous building of which he had dreamed. A flight of 365 steps, one for each day in the year, leads up to the gallery. The painted frieze below was the work of Constantine Brumidi, one of the many colorful geniuses who gave the best years of their lives to the building of Washington.

Brumidi, an Italian artist, came to America seeking liberty. He became a loyal, patriotic citizen with only one great desire—that he might live long enough to beautify the Capitol "of the one country on earth in which there is liberty." This wish was granted. Brumidi had worked at decorating various rooms in the Capitol building for more than 30 years and was almost 80 years of age when his death occurred. He was engaged in painting the unusual frieze around the rotunda walls, 75 feet above the floor, when a piece of the scaffolding on which he was standing broke loose. This gave him a severe shock from which he never recovered. Brumidi had designed the entire frieze, but the painting is only now being completed, for not until recently was it possible to find an artist whose style of work matched that of Brumidi. Allen Cox of New York is engaged on the task.

South of the rotunda is Statuary Hall, formerly the Representatives' Chamber. Each state in the Union has contributed a statue of one of its most outstanding citizens. Oklahoma sent the statue of Sequoya, a famous Indian, the inventor of the Cherokee alphabet; California sent the statue of a Spanish Franciscan priest, Father Junipero Serra, who established many of the California missions; Illinois sent the only statue of a woman, Frances Willard, founder of the Women's Christian Temperance Union.

At one place in Statuary Hall a whisper can be clearly heard across the room, and a normal tone at this spot produces a distinct echo. On one occasion when ex-President John Quincy Adams, who served as a representative for many years, was making a speech before the House, he suddenly stopped talking, turned, and looked angrily around the room. Seeing that all were quiet and orderly, Adams resumed his talk, but he again stopped and stood in indignant silence.

"Proceed, Mr. Adams," said the Speaker of the House.

John Quincy Adams who was known for his hot temper, replied, "How can I continue with my speech when some ill-mannered fellow constantly interrupts me?" It was Adams' first experience with the echo.

The Representatives' Chamber in the south wing is the largest legislative hall in the world. On the wall behind the Speaker's desk hangs the American flag, and at either side of it are full-length portraits of Washington and Lafayette. The flag is the symbol of national authority, but there is another emblem of governmental power here —the Mace which is used *only* in the House of Representatives. The Mace is patterned after the fasces which were carried by certain officials of ancient Rome. It consists of a bundle of thirteen ebony rods, enwrapped with a narrow silver band. It is 46 inches high and is topped by a silver globe bearing a silver eagle with outstretched wings.

On each day that the House is in session, promptly at noon when the Speaker takes his place, the Sergeant-at-arms, or an assistant, places the Mace on a pedestal of green Vermont marble at the right of the Speaker's desk. It remains in sight throughout the session. But when a debate becomes too heated or the members grow quarrelsome, the Speaker may give the order "PRESENT THE MACE!" Then the Sergeant-at-arms holds the Mace directly in front of the offenders. Usually, this act silences the men, but occasionally when tempers flare high, the Sergeant-at-arms may have to hold the Mace high and parade through the aisles to bring order. The last instance of this power of the Mace occurred in the late 1880's when Congressman James B. Weaver of Bloomfield, Iowa, was called to order by this emblem of authority.

The main aisle through the well of the House is the dividing line for the political parties; the Democrats sit on the Speaker's right and the Republicans on his left. The representatives occupy benches and have no desks.

The north wing of the Capitol is the Senate wing. The senators turned their original chamber over to the Supreme Court and moved into the new north wing of the Capitol building in 1859. There the senators have individual desks and chairs.

At noon each day during the session, the Vice-President (or the presiding officer of the Senate) and the Chaplain ascend the dais. The Vice-President taps the desk with the gavel and all in the room come to their feet while the Chaplain offers a prayer. The Vice-President then announces, "The Senate will be in order. The Secretary will read the journal of the last legislative day's proceedings"; thus the United States' Senate begins its day's work.

Alert boys, over 14 and under 18 years of age, act as pages in Congress. There are 21 pages in the Senate and 41 in the House. These page boys attend school three hours a day.

One reminder of the customs of early days still exists in the august Senate Chamber. Just inside the doors, at either side of the dais, on the narrow ledge at the top of the wainscoting are two small metal boxes filled with snuff. They have been there since the room was first opened. Whether any senator of today forsakes his pipe and cigars to indulge in a clandestine pinch of snuff no one knows, but it is true that the boxes frequently have to be refilled, and the Senate recently voted to let them remain there.

On the ground floor of the Capitol are a number of offices, committee rooms, several restaurants, and barber shops. In the basement of the Capitol is the crypt, a great circular room, surrounded by a forest of columns which are the actual support of the floors above. Here, in lonely state is a famous piece of sculpture said to be too heavy for the floor of Statuary Hall. This is the work of an American sculptress, Adelaide Johnson, now living in Washington at the age of 105. Carved from a huge block of beautiful Carrara marble are the three first American suffragists: Lucretia Mott, Susan B. Anthony, and Elizabeth Cady Stanton. The figures seem to be sitting within this piece of marble, and they are often irreverently spoken of as the "Ladies of the Bath Tub." This room in the crypt, like the rotunda, was for some time occupied by stalls where women sold fruit, cakes, and liquor. It became a common loafing place for coachmen and servants of the congressmen, but after a few years Congress voted to clear out all the unwholesome businesses, which had made the room less attractive as a gathering place.

It seems that hiring government employees and putting them to work on jobs that do not exist began long ago. This story came from *The Congressional Record*. In the basement below the ground floor of the Capitol is the crypt, and in the floor of the crypt is a marble star which marks the exact center of the Capitol building. Directly beneath this star is a small room which was built for the tombs of George and Martha Washington. A well-like opening was made in the floor of the rotunda above. From there it would have been possible to look down on their sarcophagi, as one may view Napoleon's tomb in the Hôtel des Invalides in Paris. But the Washington family would not permit the removal of the bodies from Mount Vernon. However, acting with unusual speed, Congress had already appointed a keeper at an annual salary of $1500, to guard the tomb, even though it was empty. This guard remained on duty until death relieved him; then a second keeper of the crypt took charge. After him a third guard served until, during the Civil War, an end was put to this easy job. Now the tomb contains only the black catafalque used at state funerals held in the Capitol.

The Capitol building was put to various uses during the War between the States. It became a real citadel where soldiers were quartered; in the basement supplies were stored and a great wholesale bakery was established. Fearing that the enemy might take the flour made in the Georgetown mills, the Union leaders sent numbers of soldiers with wagons, coaches, carts, vehicles of every sort, even barges and boats, to haul the thousands of barrels of flour to safe quarters in Washington. They were stored in the basements of the Treasury, the Post Office, and the Capitol. Immense ovens were built in the vaults under the Capitol and hundreds of bakers and yeast makers worked day and night to keep the Army and the citizens supplied with bread.

There are 430 rooms in the Capitol. Many of them are handsomely decorated and furnished, such as the Senate reception room, or the marble room, and the President's room. When visiting the Capitol, it is worth while to take a tour of the building with a guide. For a small fee, the guide will explain in detail the wonders of this, the greatest of all capitols.

One place in the United States where our flag flies continuously is on the Capitol building. During World War I, many people requested that the nation's flag be flown constantly over all the government buildings in Washington. The authorities decided that the Capitol was the appropriate place and from that time on, over both the east and west fronts of the Capitol, our flag has floated day and night. In only one other spot is the flag always displayed. This is over the grave of Francis Scott Key, author of "The Star-Spangled Banner," at Frederick, Maryland.

Outside the Capitol building, at the northeast corner of the Plaza, is the Senate Office Building. Each Senator has three large rooms where he and his staff carry on the business of their important positions. Here are a number of committee rooms, lounges, and also a large restaurant. An underground passage, equipped with a little electric railway for the convenience of the senators, leads from this building to the Capitol.

At the southeast and southwest corners of the Capitol Plaza, across Independence Avenue, are two large marble buildings known as the old and new House Office Buildings. These are the representatives' offices, not quite as roomy and elaborate as the senatorial quarters. An underground passage, with a ramp instead of a railroad, leads from the House offices to the Capitol.

# On Capitol Hill

## The Library of Congress

East of the Capitol across the Plaza on the right, is a gray granite structure with a low green dome. This is the Congressional Library, the largest library in the world.

When the United States Government moved from Philadelphia to Washington, the 950 books and nine maps belonging to Congress were placed in a small room in the new Capitol building. This library had grown to more than 3,000 volumes when it was destroyed at the time the Capitol was burned by the British in 1814. Then about 6,750 books were purchased from Thomas Jefferson to form a nucleus of another library. It grew so rapidly that there were a million volumes to be moved from the crowded Capitol to the new library building in 1897. In June, 1952 the total number of books in the Congressional Library was 30,746,772.

The Library of Congress is an elaborately decorated building; the works of 50 of America's foremost artists and sculptors adorn the structure. In front, in the niches under the steps, is Neptune's fountain. There the king of the sea is seated on his throne surrounded by his court: nymphs on their sea horses, lordly Triton blowing his shell trumpet, pop-eyed frogs, huge turtles, and even a sea serpent. All of these, in a rocky grotto under cascades of clear, sparkling water, are a refreshing sight on a hot summer day.

From the top of the outside stairs there is a fine view of the Capitol. Sculptured busts of the great in literature and carved heads of the various races of mankind are on the outer walls. Magnificent bronze doors open into the great hall, the grandest of all the lobbies in the capital city. There is beauty, from the marble floor, inlaid with polished brass figures of the zodiac, to the vaulted roof, 72 feet above. Countless stories are told in the handsome mural paintings. At either side of the hall is a marble stairway with a balustrade carved like no other in the world. The arts, science, and industry are represented by the chubby figures of baby boys: A tiny soldier wears a helmet, an astronomer peers through a telescope, a small gardener is shown with hoe and rake, a fat little cook watches a bubbling kettle, and there are others equally entrancing. On the second floor is the Gutenberg Bible, the first book printed from movable type by the fifteenth century German printer by whose named it is identified.

The main reading room, seen from the gallery above, is an impressive sight. There is rich color everywhere, from the brilliant stained glass in the dome and the bronze statues below the arched windows, to the varied background of the book-lined alcoves and the red, brown, and yellows of the polished marble pillars. In this vast rotunda there are enough desks and chairs to accommodate 1,000 readers at one time.

When a reader presents a ticket requesting a book, a clerk at the central desk inserts the slip into a small container and pops it into a pneumatic tube which whisks it away to a messenger among the book stacks on floors above or below. Soon the book appears on an electrically operated conveyor, from which a messenger delivers it to the reader's desk. Volumes wanted by congressmen are shot to the Capitol through an underground brick tunnel, large enough for a man to walk in. An endless cable conveyor carries the books from the terminal in the Library basement through the large tube under the Plaza to the receiving room in the Capitol, a quarter of a mile away. In a few minutes the books are delivered to the congressman who had asked for them.

There are many divisions in this great library. From the nine maps in the original Congressional Library has developed one of the largest cartographic collections to be found anywhere in the world. There is a rare book room where precious old volumes are kept in dust-proof, air-cooled shelves and cases. The irreplaceable volumes purchased from Thomas Jefferson are preserved here. There is a Fine Arts Department with collections of prints, old and new, etchings, photographs, and other works of art. In the periodical reading room are all the current magazines, technical publications, and almost everyone's home town newspaper. There are thousands of books and publications in Braille for the blind. In the music division are the scores of folk tunes, operas, and a marvelous assortment of phonograph records. There is also a collection of rare musical instruments, including the Betts Stradivarius which is said to be the most perfect violin, as well as one of the most valuable, in the world.

Vast as the Library of Congress seemed in 1897, it soon became overcrowded and in 1938 another huge building, the Annex, was constructed on the east, across "B" Street from the main Library.

This stately Annex, of Georgia marble, is less ornate

than the main Library, but it is grand in its simplicity. It will hold 12,000,000 books and it contains 172 study rooms.

Although the Library of Congress was originally intended for the sole use of congressmen and government officials, this institution serves other libraries, colleges, and the general public. Here hundreds of writers and research workers take advantage of the valuable material which is offered without any charge.

### The Folger Library

Across the corner from the great Library of Congress, at the left of the Annex, is the Folger Library. This is of great interest to all lovers and students of Shakespeare.

Henry Clay Folger, a wealthy businessman of New York, had an unusual hobby. During his student days at Amherst College, he had become a great admirer of Shakespeare's writings. This led to a desire to collect not only the works of Shakespeare but the art, music, other literature—everything connected with the great poet and the times in which he lived. Mrs. Folger, a Vassar graduate, shared her husband's enthusiasm and for more than 50 years this Shakespearean collection was the chief interest in the lives of these two people.

The collection finally became so valuable that much of it was stored in safety deposit vaults. Then the Folgers decided to make it available to the public. England was eager to give the collection a home in Stratford-on-Avon, where Shakespeare was born, but Henry Folger was determined to give his treasures to his own country. He presented this gift—the greatest ever given for purely literary research—to Washington, D.C., stating that his earnest desire was "to help make the United States a center for literary study and progress." Amherst College, Folger's alma mater, has charge of administering the funds left for the upkeep and management of the beautiful building and its contents.

The marble structure with its classic lines is in perfect harmony with its massive neighbors, and the grounds, artistically landscaped, make an emerald setting for the snowy building. In the foreground, poised on the rim of a fountain, is the figure of Puck—his hands upraised in mock horror as, with an impish grin, he seems to repeat his lines from *A Midsummer Night's Dream:* "Lord, what fools these mortals be!"

With the opening of the doors, 400 years seem to roll back and a setting of the sixteenth century is revealed. Playbills, jewels, gloves, costumes, music scores, and countless priceless souvenirs of the matchless Shakespeare and those far-away days fill the cases in the great exhibition hall. The Globe Theater is there, a small model of course, where the first performances of Shakespeare's plays were produced. Against the wall stands a centuries-old tall grandfather's clock, keeping perfect time in spite of its years. There are thousands of relics, even a corset worn by Queen Elizabeth I but this is modestly hidden away in a vault in the basement. At the east end of the building there is a real theater, exactly like those of Shakespeare's day; but it is an exclusive one, seating only 262 persons.

The reading room and library are copies of rooms in ancient British castles. The books—85,000 of them—are of almost unbelievable value. One book of poems printed in 1599 cost $75,000. Some of these volumes were so valuable that they were sent from New York to Washington in an armored car with five guards.

Anyone is welcome to visit the Folger Library, but only accredited scholars and students of Shakespeare are allowed the privileges of study and research here.

### The Supreme Court Building

The classic white temple on First Street, north of the Library of Congress, is the Supreme Court Building. Tons and tons of marble were used in its construction, more marble, it is said, than in any building in the world. Carved friezes adorn the exterior walls, and giant sculptured figures are at either side of the wide, marble stairways, each representing a story from the world of legal science.

The exterior of the building is of Vermont and Georgia marble; Alabama marble has been used for the interior. The 36 huge columns in the main corridor are unusual, as each is one solid piece of marble. They were quarried in Alabama, shaped and polished in Tennessee, then loaded separately—only one to a flat car—and carefully shipped to Washington.

At the end of this broad corridor is the real heart of the building: the Supreme Court Chamber where the nine Justices, the highest court of the land, administer "equal justice under law." The Court Chamber is not large, but it is impressive. The columns of colorful Italian marble, the walls of ivory vein marble from Spain, the gleaming bronze gates, the dark mahogany furniture, and the crimson velvet curtains all give it an air of rich elegance. Handsome mahogany chairs were provided for the Justices, but they preferred to have their old ones brought over from the Court room in the Capitol. Some of these chairs have low backs, some have high ones, and one has a pillow headrest. But they add a human touch to the grand room, and their owners are satisfied with them.

There are four broad marble stairways in the building, and two of them are of unusual construction: they are elliptical spirals, extending for five stories from the basement to the third floor, with no visible supports. The steps are keyed together by being overlapped and having the inner ends deeply inserted into the marble wall. The bronze balustrades of an intricate design add to the beauty of the stairways.

The third floor, devoted to the law library, contains no marble; it is made entirely of wood. The walls, tables, and other furniture are all of carved American white oak.

The Supreme Court convenes the first Monday in October and sits through to the following June. The opening of the daily session is interesting and impressive. At noon, promptly on the stroke of twelve, the court crier announces the Justices: "The Honorable Chief Justice and Associate Justices of the Supreme Court of the United States." The audience rises, the red curtains part, and the nine black-robed Justices take their places. The crier then voices the ancient court call which is said to have been derived from that used in England since the time of William the Conqueror: "Oyez, Oyez, Oyez! All persons having business before the Honorable, the Supreme Court of the United States, are admonished to draw near and give their attention, for the Court is now sitting. God save the United States and this Honorable Court."

# *The Mall*

In the new city of Washington, in the early 1800's, people found it hard to believe that the Mall, as L'Enfant had named it, could ever be anything but a swampy, weedy waste. It was just a sloping hillside covered with briars and underbrush, topped by tall trees and ending in a broad marsh. Tiber Creek, coming in from the Maryland hills, sprawled along the north side; James Creek wriggled through the alders on the south, and at high tide the Potomac River crept out of its banks to refill the ponds and puddles near the shore.

For many years no attempt was made to improve the area. In 1835 the Baltimore and Ohio Railroad came to town, laid its tracks up the Mall, and built a depot in front of the Capitol grounds where the Peace Monument now stands. The Pennsylvania Railroad later located its station farther west on the Mall, near Sixth Street. Some of the marsh was drained, and the Tiber was walled up and made into a canal. The Smithsonian Institution was the first permanent building on the Mall, and the Washington Monument was the second structure.

During the Civil War, military camps and hospitals spread over this open space. Tiber Creek, or Canal, became a filthy cesspool. The Mall was the city's dumping ground where goats, pigs, poultry, and other livestock wandered at will among the rubbish piles. The west end of this beauty spot-to-be, between the Washington Monument and the Potomac River, was the largest marsh in the District.

Early in 1871 the canal was filled in and the Mall's worst nuisance was removed. But it was the capital city's first centennial that brought it a new era.

In 1900, on the one hundredth anniversary of the occupation of Washington by the Government, President McKinley called the governors of all the states to the capital. Congress held appropriate exercises. There was a great civic parade, and everyone was heartily ashamed of the Mall. The members of the American Institute of Architects, convening at that time, were disgusted at the hodgepodge appearance of the city. They wrote papers on the subject of the needed improvements in Washington, went home, and nothing happened.

Then Senator McMillan, Chairman of the District of Columbia Commissioners, decided that he would do something about the matter. McMillan was a man of wealth and high ideals. He gave generously of his time and money to originate a plan for developing Washington on a scale fully as grand as that envisioned by Washington, Jefferson, and L'Enfant. He appointed a board of five men, the best known architects, artists, and sculptors in America at that time. The senator even advanced the necessary funds to send this committee abroad to visit the famous cities and capitals of Europe—Paris, Rome, Budapest, and Vienna.

The members of the commission returned home fully realizing the grandeur of L'Enfant's plans, and resolved

to execute them. They were the first, since Washington
and Jefferson, to grasp the Frenchman's vision of our nation's capital. Daniel Burnham, the Chicago architect
who was chairman of the commission, wrote the following
words of advice to the committee when they began their
work of improving the capital:

"Make no little plans; they have no magic to stir men's
blood, and probably themselves will not be realized. Make
big plans; aim high in hope and work, remembering that
a noble, logical diagram once recorded will never die, but
long after we are gone will be a living thing, asserting itself with ever-growing insistency. Remember that our sons
and grandsons are going to do things that would stag-
ger us. Let your watchword be order and your beacon
beauty."

The first step, the commissioners decided, was to clear
away the railroad tracks and depots from the Mall and so
restore the open vista from the Capitol to the Potomac.

A suitable site a half mile northwest from the Capitol
was selected for the Union Station, the first building
erected by the McMillan Commission. The tracks of the
southern railways were enclosed in two great tubes, 40 feet
below the surface, extending for a mile under First Street,
from Neptune's fountain in front of the Library of Congress, down to the terminal behind the railroad station.
The remaining tracks, entering the city from the north,
west, and east, were cleverly led by inconspicuous ways to
the yards in the rear of the Union Station. Slowly, L'Enfant's vision of the beautiful city began to take shape.

L'Enfant had planned a large open plaza, similar to the
one at the east entrance of the Capitol, at the head of
the Mall, directly west of the Capitol grounds. Instead,
the space is called Union Square, and it contains several
thoroughfares and some outstanding memorials and stat-

ues. The Peace Monument is at the northeast corner, the
Garfield statue is at the southeast corner of this area,
while the Grant Memorial is in the center, at the head of
the Mall. The monument to Grant is one of the world's
largest equestrian statues, second only to that of Victor
Emmanuel in Rome, which is only six inches higher than
the Grant Memorial.

L'Enfant had compared his plan for the center of the
capital city to two axes, crossing at the point he marked
for the monument to George Washington. The east-west
axis began at the Capitol and ended at the Potomac
River. The north-south axis began at the President's Palace and terminated at the south on the Potomac. L'Enfant
indicated that monuments should be placed at the west
and south ends of the axes, and there the Lincoln and the
Jefferson Memorials now stand.

The Mall, a broad, grassy parkway, extends down the
main axis, beginning at the foot of the Capitol grounds.
Government buildings line either side of the Mall.

### The Botanic Gardens

Down the Mall from the Capitol, at the corner of First
Street and Independence Avenue, Northwest, are the
Botanic Gardens. Hundreds of unusual plants can be seen
here—exotic blossoms from the tropics, weird desert
flowers, and rare aquatic plants. Various flower shows—of
azaleas, chrysanthemums, and others in their seasons—are
arranged for interested visitors, and there is no charge for
admission.

George Washington and Thomas Jefferson were ardent
flower-lovers, and naturally, when planning the capital,
Washington suggested a botanic garden. But it was not
until 50 years later that one was established.

### The Federal Security Building

This huge building is just west of the Botanic Gardens on Independence Avenue. It houses a number of agencies organized by the Government to promote social and economic security, educational opportunities, and the health of the nation's citizens. Among these agencies are the Social Security Administration, the Office of Education, the Public Health Service, the Children's Bureau, and the Food and Drug Administration.

### The Army Medical Museum

The dark red building on the northwest corner of Independence Avenue and Seventh Street is of importance to members of the medical and dental professions. It is often classed as a part of the Smithsonian Institution, but does not actually belong to that group.

Here is the most comprehensive library on the subjects of medicine and surgery to be found in the world. This library was organized with the surplus money given by the hospitals after the Civil War. The museum contains thousands upon thousands of specimens and exhibits of wounds and diseases resulting from warfare. The instruments and the methods of surgery used from ancient times to the present day are on display.

The building has long been outgrown and outmoded, and will soon be replaced.

### The Smithsonian Institution

One of the greatest educational organizations of the world, this institution was given to the United States by an Englishman, James Smithson, a wealthy scientist, who left his fortune of more than half a million dollars to a country which he had never seen. He directed that the money be used to found an establishment "for the increase and diffusion of knowledge among men," which he requested be called the "Smithsonian Institution."

The dark red, sandstone Institution, between Ninth and Eleventh Streets on the Mall, contrasts in color and style of architecture with other buildings in the vicinity. The turrets and towers resemble the ancient castles in the homeland of the English donor.

The Smithsonian, which was begun in 1846, was the first building on the Mall. Here are the administrative offices of the publications, library, research divisions, and other departments of the great institution. Educators, explorers, hunters, and specialists in all lines are sent to various parts of the world to collect information and specimens for the Smithsonian. Archaeology, ethnology, geology—all the "ologies" and sciences—are studied by the experts of this super-institution of learning.

In the Graphic Arts Section is a complete exhibit of all of the processes of the different methods of illustrating. Lithography, etching, photography, engraving, printing —all are described, with examples of the work at various stages. Benjamin Franklin's printing press is here; also that famous piece of engraving, the Lord's Prayer on an area the size of a needle's eye.

A tour through the Arts and Industries Building is as educational as a visit to a world's fair. There, more than 121,000 specimens of interest to children and adults are displayed. The first hall is devoted to exhibits which bring our country's history to life. Suspended from the ceiling is the tiny plane in which Charles A. Lindbergh made the first nonstop flight alone across the Atlantic. The huge, broad-striped flag upon which Francis Scott

Key gazed when he wrote our "Star-Spangled Banner" hangs on one wall in this room.

Girls like to see the gowns worn by the former ladies of the White House, while the boys prefer the guns and other weapons of warfare. The uniforms worn by General Washington in the Revolutionary War, by the soldiers in the Mexican, Civil, Spanish-American, and World Wars are found here. The great contrast between the old and the modern uniforms is shown by the shiny helmets topped with bright plumes, and by the scarlet coats, so brilliant when compared with the khaki, olive drab, and other dull shades worn by the fighting men of today. The weapons and artillery of the past seem ineffective to eyes accustomed to the bombs, powerful tanks, and planes of this era. Progress in transportation is represented by all sorts of conveyances, from their crudest beginnings to this year's newest models. There are ships, ancient and modern, for those who have the sea in their blood. No matter what the subject of one's special interest, its history and progress are almost certain to be shown here.

In this vast exhibition hall there is one group of living workers actively engaged in the manufacture of their product. Hundreds of tiny Italian honeybees, busy in a large glass hive, demonstrate the process of honey-making.

An extra exhibit of all modes of air travel, from kites and balloons to today's latest war planes, may be seen in the small aircraft building nearby.

There is also a little building devoted to astrophysics, the study of the moon, stars, and other heavenly bodies.

*The Freer Gallery.* This art collection was the gift of Charles Freer to the Smithsonian Institution. Charles Lang Freer, a Detroit businessman, contributed his collection of the paintings of outstanding American artists, including most of Whistler's works, as well as his extensive accumulation of Oriental arts and rare manuscripts. In addition to the collections, the gift included a model gallery in which to house and display them, and $1,000,000 to maintain the building and collection.

In the Whistler collection the famous peacock room is a most popular one; it has an interesting history: James Abbott McNeill Whistler was an American artist, eccentric in manner and dress. At one time Whistler was employed in the offices of the Navy Department in Washington. However, he preferred to pose as an Englishman and spent most of his time in that country. After decorating a dining room for a wealthy client, Whistler had a disagreement with him over the bill. He had agreed to do the work for $2,500, but he had sent a bill for $10,000. Mr. Leyland, his patron, declared the charge was exorbitant and refused to pay it. Whistler finally received only $1,000. He was indignant and, in revenge, painted two extra peacocks on the wall. One, an arrogant bird with gold pieces all over it, represented Mr. Leyland; the other, a meek, humble peacock, was supposedly Whistler. At least that was Whister's characterization of the two birds.

Mr. Freer purchased the entire room—ceiling, walls, and furniture—and brought it from England to his Detroit home. After his death it came to the Freer Gallery.

*The National Museum of Natural History.* This gray granite building is across the Mall from the red sandstone buildings of the Smithsonian Institution.

In the bird hall there are thousands of specimens, birds from every part of the world. Not far away are the terrifying monsters that lived in ages past, with names as odd and almost as long as the animals themselves. For instance, there is the giant Diplodocus, "70 feet long and 12 feet high," and the "three-horned Triceratops." They were real once upon a time, but today they look like figures in a nightmare.

Life-sized figures of Indians and Eskimos, dressed in their native costumes, are shown working at the various tasks of their daily life.

There are interesting displays of minerals and precious gems—colored diamonds and one huge black diamond. The National Collection of Fine Arts contains rare pieces of sculpture, paintings, tapestries, and other treasures.

Perhaps the most popular department of the Smithsonian Institution is the zoo with its collection of thousands of interesting living creatures, but to see that one must go out to Rock Creek Park on Connecticut Avenue.

### The National Gallery of Art

One of the newest and most beautiful buildings in the city, the National Gallery of Art faces the Mall and Constitution Avenue between Fourth and Seventh Streets. Andrew W. Mellon, a former Secretary of the Treasury, presented his extensive collection of masterpieces of painting and sculpture to the city of Washington and also donated $15,000,000 for the building. The rose-white Tennessee marble used in the exterior is gradually shaded, darkest at the base of the structure, giving an unusual effect. The National Gallery is one of the largest marble buildings in the world.

Twenty-four columns of dark green Italian marble encircle the large central rotunda on the main floor, and in the center is a magnificent fountain topped by a graceful bronze figure of Mercury. Both the east and west wings terminate in the garden court which contains fountains, flowers, and comfortable benches.

Many people ask why the gallery is not called "the Mellon Gallery." It was Mr. Mellon's desire to make this a *national* gallery accessible to all who wished to contribute works of art to it, and not to limit it to his personal collections. In this beautiful building he planned a gallery with enough space to accommodate many collections besides his own. Already numerous gifts have been received; among them are the famous collection of paintings and sculpture of the Italian schools, contributed by Mr. Samuel H. Kress, the Widener collection, and the gift of Mr. Lessing J. Rosenwald. While the National Gallery is classed as a part of the Smithsonian Institution, it is directly controlled by a board of trustees headed by the Chief Justice of the United States, the Secretary of State, and the Secretary of the Treasury.

The finest examples of every branch of art are displayed in this gallery: painting, sculpture, prints, drawings, jewelry, porcelains, tapestries—and all exhibits are open to the public with no charge for admission.

The Andrew W. Mellon Memorial Fountain is directly opposite the National Gallery of Art at the intersection of Pennsylvania and Constitution Avenues and Sixth Street. At a cost of more than $300,000, this memorial to the founder of the National Gallery of Art was given to the Federal Government. All of the funds were contributed by loyal personal friends of Mr. Mellon. At the dedication ceremony on May 9, 1952, the fountain was turned over to the Secretary of the Interior for operation by the National Park Service.

The fountain consists of three tiers of basins cast in bronze. Water from the tall, sparkling plume falls into the two top basins, then into the largest one at the base. The twelve signs of the zodiac have been cast in high relief on the fluted wall of this last basin.

A granite walk, 7 feet wide, surrounds the magnificent fountain, and west of the fountain, along this walk, is a granite seat, 25 feet in length. Carved in the center of its back are the words:

1855   Andrew W. Mellon   1937
Financier   Industrialist   Statesman
Secretary of the Treasury 1921-1932
Ambassador to Great Britain 1932-1933
Founder of the National Gallery of Art 1937
This Fountain is a Tribute from His Friends

## The Department of Agriculture

This building faces the Mall and Independence Avenue between Fourteenth and Fifteenth Streets. The function of this department is the collection and distribution of information on all agricultural subjects. A surprisingly large number of branches and bureaus are included in this agency, for their work is essential not alone to farmers, but to the life and health of all the citizens of the nation.

Thomas Jefferson might well be called the first "field man" in this department, for he collected and brought home seeds, bulbs, and even cuttings of flowers and shrubs from all the foreign countries he visited. The finest rice grown in the United States came from a pocketful gathered by Jefferson in Italy and sent back to South Carolina. George Washington, an enthusiastic farmer, called the attention of the very first Congress to the importance of agriculture in the development of our country.

When the United States was 40 years old, Congress voted to give $1,000 to the Commissioner of Patents with which to buy seeds for distribution to the farmers. But it was not until the administration of President Lincoln that an independent Department of Agriculture was created. A Commissioner of Agriculture was appointed, who, with a staff of 73, occupied a small building on the Mall, and carried on necessary experiments on a 40 acre field.

The work of this department was under the supervision

of the Secretary of Agriculture who was given a place in the President's Cabinet. Lands, foods, forests, public roads, home economics, animals, plants, and all their diseases and cures, weather reports, and innumerable miscellaneous items make up the list of subjects studied by this department. The extent of the department's research is world-wide. American plant hunters have traveled on every continent to bring back hardy plants—alfalfa, Sudan grass, and disease-resistant grains. Other workers seek parasites which will destroy the insects attacking fruit or grain. Thousands of people are now employed by the United States Department of Agriculture in the capital and all parts of our country.

Two huge white marble buildings on the Mall are occupied by the offices of the Department of Agriculture, the largest governmental agency established for scientific research. It is, in fact, the largest organization in the world entirely devoted to the science of agriculture.

### The Bureau of Engraving and Printing

At Fourteenth and C Streets is one of the most important buildings in Washington. Its products are vital to all America, in fact to the whole world; for it is here that the United States' "paper money" is made—millions and millions of dollars every day. It is fascinating to watch sheets of white paper passing from one machine to another, finally appearing as valuable currency. Government checks, certificates, bonds, and postage stamps are also designed and printed in this, one of the finest plants of its kind.

Ink, in the many shades and colors necessary for currency, certificates, and drafts, is manufactured in this establishment in unbelievably huge quantities. Even the gum used on the back of the stamps is made here. It is not mucilage, as many suppose, but is a gum prepared from the root of the cassava plant which is also the source of the familiar tapioca pudding.

This "money factory" is a division of the Treasury Department and its invaluable contents are protected by the efficient Treasury guards. At night this building can easily be distinguished from all others by the bluish-green lights from the thousands of windows and their colorful reflections in the placid waters of the Tidal Basin nearby.

CHAPTER

 5

# The Washington Monument and the Lincoln Memorial

## The Washington National Monument

From every part of Washington and from many miles around the great obelisk can be seen towering against the sky. It is the tallest work of masonry in the world—555 feet, 5⅛ inches in height. Yet, unbelievable as it seems, this monument was once stolen and kept out of the hands of the Washington National Monument Society for almost two years.

In 1783, a month before the signing of the final treaty between the United States and England, Congress voted to erect an equestrian statue in honor of George Washington, the hero of the Revolution. Being a modest man, and knowing exactly how little money there was in the new country, Washington opposed the idea of a statue of himself. Instead, he suggested the building of an obelisk to commemorate the War for Independence. L'Enfant marked the location for the monument on the Mall. It was to be at the junction of the imaginary east and west line drawn through the dome of the Capitol, and the meridian line north and south through the President's Palace. Thomas Jefferson placed a small mound of stones to mark the exact spot.

Soon after the end of the Revolutionary War, Congress voted to erect an equestrian statue on the Mall in honor of George Washington, but nothing more was done about it until Washington's death on December 14, 1799, when gratitude flamed again. Once more Congress voted to build a monument in Washington's honor and to use it as a burial place for the hero's body. However, that plan could not be carried out as Washington had stated in his will that he wished to be buried at Mount Vernon. Time and again, Congress brought up the matter of the Washington Monument, but money was still scarce and no definite measures were taken.

In 1833 a group of citizens organized the Washington National Monument Society. They called on artists to submit designs for a suitable monument, and selected the plan offered by Robert Mills. This was to be a hollow, marble shaft, 600 feet in height, mounted on a circular colonnade 100 feet from the ground. On the top of this columned temple a 30 foot statue of Washington, draped in a Roman toga, was to stand in a chariot, driving three spans of prancing horses. Fortunately, this bizarre plan was finally reduced to the beautiful simple obelisk, a design most appropriate to the dignity of the Father of His Country.

Raising the money for the monument was difficult. Americans everywhere were asked to contribute to the fund. Women held fairs and bazaars. School children gave their pennies. Small models of the monument were placed in stores and other public places with slotted boxes beside them for contributions. After $70,000 had been collected the cornerstone was laid, on July 4, 1848. The Masonic order of ceremonies was followed, and the same silver trowel which had been used by George Washington in laying the Capitol cornerstone again served. The original spot selected by Major L'Enfant was such a marshy place that the foundation was laid on a slight knoll 300 feet to the southwest.

Blocks of marble and other fine stone appropriately carved and inscribed were contributed by the states, by colleges, churches, Indian tribes, many foreign countries, and interested individuals. These were to line the inner walls of the structure. Pope Pius IX sent a block of marble from the Temple of Concord in Rome, and that gift caused an unfortunate incident. A political group, anti-Catholic and anti-foreign, calling itself the "American Party" but commonly spoken of as the "Know Nothings," was bitterly opposed to the use of the Pope's block of marble. One night, some members of this organization overpowered the guard at the monument and stole this marble block. It was believed that they broke it into pieces which they threw into the Potomac, as this block was never seen again. This angered a great many people and put a stop to all contributions—money as well as tribute blocks.

Not content with this unpardonable act, the "Know Nothings" committed one even more disgraceful. They took possession of the buildings on the monument grounds and all the papers relating to structure. They then announced that they were in charge and would build the Washington Monument "for Americans and by Americans." All of their bold talk amounted to nothing, however. They collected no funds, and the whole organization disbanded in less than two years' time. The monument was then returned to the care of the society. But before any of their plans could be carried out, the Civil War came on. For sixteen years the Washington Monument stood 152 feet high, abandoned by everyone.

When General Grant became President, after the end of the war, he instructed Congress to appropriate sufficient money to complete the monument and assigned Colonel Thomas F. Casey with a detail of Army men to take charge of the work. Then another difficulty arose; the structure was found to be tilting slightly to one side. The engineers decided that the foundation was too shallow, and that a broader, deeper base was necessary. By digging under the foundation, a small section at a time, then filling the excavation in with stone, rubble, and concrete as a deep underpinning, an adequate groundwork was provided with no damage to the monument. This was such a difficult piece of work, and the method was so unusual that engineers from all parts of the United States, and even from foreign countries, came to watch the work as it was being done.

The monument is built of white marble from Massachusetts and Maryland. Short lightning rods were placed around the top of the shaft, and it is said that each rod was tipped with platinum. The capstone was set December 6, 1884. It was topped by an aluminum peak bearing the Latin inscription, *Laus Deo* ("Praise to God"). (During World War II, there was a scarcity of this metal, and this aluminum cap was removed and used for plane production.) The monument was dedicated on February 21, 1885, and was formally opened to the public on October 9, 1888 —just 105 years after Congress first voted to build the statue of George Washington.

Inside the shaft an iron stairway of 898 steps with 50

landings enables one to read the inscriptions on the 202 tribute blocks lining the monument. But with less effort an elevator ride of 70 seconds brings one to a marvelous view of the symmetrical plan of the city. It is advisable to ride up and walk down the stairs.

About 30 acres are included in the grounds. At the southeast end of the grassy slope is a natural amphitheater, called the Sylvan Theater, where plays and concerts offer entertainment to thousands on warm summer evenings.

Ever so often the mystery of the underground monument bobs up. Usually a taxi driver or some bystander points out a large iron manhole cover half hidden in the grass about 50 feet south of the Washington Monument. The curious sightseer raises the cover and finds that there is a little monument down in that brick-lined well. What is it? Why is it there? The answer is simple. This miniature monument, 15 feet high, is technically known as a "bench mark," and it is used to check any settlement or change in the earth's surface near the great monument.

The surface of the Washington Monument had its first cleaning in 1934; it was scrubbed with wire brushes dipped in water and sand. A steel scaffolding was erected around it for the use of the workers during the cleaning operation. And at some time during the five months it was there, it was reported that someone climbed up and stole the platinum tips from the 144 lightning rods placed around the top of the monument.

Floodlights installed about the grounds make the monument plainly visible by night, and red lights illuminate the top of the shaft, to prevent accidents to planes flying by night.

This noble monument, erected in honor of the great George Washington, is the Capital's most distinctive landmark.

## The Reflecting Pool

Between the Washington Monument and the Lincoln Memorial lies the Reflecting Pool—a strip of shining water 2,000 feet long and 160 feet wide. The stately obelisk and the marble temple are faithfully mirrored on its calm surface. In direct contrast, is a small transverse pool near the Washington Monument where 200 jets throw the water high, then down into the pool in sprays rainbow-tinted from the refracted sunlight. At night, at certain times, colored lights are played on the sprays with beautiful effect.

## The Lincoln Memorial

Standing alone, apart from the business and turmoil of the city, at the end of the Mall, is the beautiful Lincoln Memorial.

Two years after Abraham Lincoln's death plans were begun to erect a monument in honor of the martyred President; but not until 57 years had passed was the magnificent memorial formally dedicated.

There was much discussion over the nature of a fitting tribute to Lincoln's memory. One of the most popular ideas was that of a Lincoln Memorial Highway extending from Washington, D.C., to the Gettysburg battle fields and on to the Pacific Coast. Other people were in favor of some kind of a monument in the capital, comparable to the Washington Monument. But no plan for this was adopted until 1901. Then the McMillan Park Commission decided to extend the Mall three quarters of a mile by filling in the swamp lands between the Washington Monument and the Potomac River. There, at the end of the Mall, in line with the Capitol and the Washington Monument, the Commissioners decided, was the ideal place for the Lincoln Monument.

Violent objections arose over the choice of this site. Speaker Joseph Cannon, a member of the Lincoln Memorial Committee, was quoted as saying, "Don't put the memorial here, boys. Why, the malarial ague from these mosquitoes would shake it to pieces!" Some people said that it was too far from the center of the city; others agreed with Cannon that a mosquito-ridden swamp was no place for a tribute to Lincoln.

Nothing further was done about the Lincoln Monument for ten years. Then President William H. Taft appointed a Fine Arts Commission with Daniel Burnham as Chairman. (Burnham was the man whose advice, "Make no little plans," was so inspiring to the first Park Commission.) The chairman announced that the Lincoln Memorial would be erected on the east bank of the Potomac, on the east and west axis of the Capitol and the Washington Monument; and that the Lincoln Memorial was to have a character essentially distinct from any monument in Washington, now or hereafter.

Henry Bacon, a New York architect, planned the building, and Daniel Chester French was the sculptor who carved the Lincoln statue. On May 30th, Memorial Day, 1922, William Howard Taft, the Chief Justice of the United States Supreme Court, made the presentation speech, turning over the Lincoln Memorial to President Harding.

The Lincoln Memorial is a stately temple built of Colorado yule marble which is noted for its fine texture and its snowy whiteness. A colonnade of 38 fluted columns surrounds the walls of the hall. On a frieze above the pillars, the names of the 36 states of the Union at the time of Lincoln's death, are inscribed; the present 48 states are named on a frieze around the top of the building. Although the ceiling is made of marble, it is translucent. This was accomplished by soaking the thin sections of the stone in melted beeswax so that the light penetrates each panel.

Marble columns divide the interior into three halls, and in the central one is the famous statue of Lincoln carved from Georgia marble. The great President is sitting in a flag-draped armchair; his eyes are sad and weary, yet far-seeing, as he gazes toward the Capitol in the distance. The following dimensions may help one to appreciate the size of this statue: the chair is 12½ feet high, the whole statue is 19 feet tall and the head is 3 feet high; the booted foot is 3½ feet long.

Lincoln's second inaugural address is engraved on the interior of the north wall; the Gettysburg Address is inscribed on the south wall; and on the west wall over his head are the words: "In this temple as in the hearts of the people for whom he saved the Union the memory of Abraham Lincoln is enshrined forever."

Everyone who comes to Washington visits the Lincoln Memorial, and all gaze upon it with awe and reverence. Truly, as Chief Justice Taft declared, "It is a shrine where all may worship."

CHAPTER

 6

## Pennsylvania Avenue

Pennsylvania Avenue extends diagonally across the city
from the southeastern limits of the District of Columbia
at Commodore Barney Circle for a distance of 7 miles
northwest, to a point beyond Rock Creek in Georgetown.
This "grand avenue," the first in the capital, was named
Pennsylvania in honor of the state which was the home
of the first Congress. It is commonly referred to as "The
Avenue" by many people in Washington.

"The Grand Avenue connecting both the palace and
the federal house will be most magnificent and most con-
venient," wrote President George Washington to Congress in 1791, in his report of L'Enfant's plan. But for
years this "grand avenue" was nothing but a narrow path
through a maze of trees, brush, and weeds, along the
marshy banks of Tiber Creek. Then a straight roadway was
cut from the Capitol to the little knoll where the President's Palace was getting under way. This was the beginning of the nation's famous Pennsylvania Avenue.

Even for years after the President's Palace and the

Capitol were built, only a plank walk—not a wide one at that—ran for some length down the center of this avenue. There were roadways on either side, muddy and rutty or dusty, according to the season of the year and the condition of the weather.

In President John Adams' time in Washington, the "grand avenue" was filled with stumps and bog holes. Several times the President's carriage became stuck in the mud and had to be pried out. For some time a stage coach ran from the President's Palace to the Capitol, at a charge of 25 cents a trip. Often Tiber Creek and the Potomac River overflowed and flooded the Avenue so that the people had to be taken up and down the street in row boats. Late in 1801 the width of the Avenue, 160 feet, was cut through from the Capitol to Fifteenth Street. A log corduroy road was laid down the center and a stone bridge built over the Tiber where it crossed Pennsylvania Avenue at Seventh Street.

President Jefferson had the Avenue graded and four rows of Lombardy poplar trees planted, thus making a three-lane highway. During Andrew Jackson's second term, a strip 80 feet wide down the center of the avenue was macadamized; Jefferson's poplar trees were removed, and elms were planted along the outer edges. It was not a grand avenue in any sense. From the Capitol down to Tenth Street, this thoroughfare was fringed with saloons, cheap show places, shoddy shops, and gambling houses.

Nevertheless, Pennsylvania Avenue has always preserved its prestige. No street in the United States is so rich in traditions of national affairs. It is called "the nation's parade ground" and "the avenue of the nation." Since Jefferson's time every inaugural procession has passed along Pennsylvania Avenue to and from the Capitol. Down its black-draped length silent multitudes have stood with bared heads and sad hearts to watch the funeral processions of the seven Presidents of the United States who have died in office. Beneath fluttering bunting and waving flags happy, shouting throngs have lined this noble avenue to welcome our returning fighting men and honor our war heroes.

The people of George Washington's time thought the crude road cut through the forest a "grand avenue." What would they think of today's stately Pennsylvania Avenue with its many impressive buildings on the Federal Triangle? This is a three-cornered piece of land between Pennsylvania and Constitution Avenues. It was formerly a boggy marsh and one of the ugliest slum spots in Washington. Now the old shacks have been cleared away and the swamp filled in and made into attractively landscaped grounds. Fine marble buildings, housing governmental departments, occupy this area.

### Federal Trade Commission

The wedge-shaped building at the apex of the Federal Triangle is occupied by the Federal Trade Commission. The function of this organization is the enforcement of fair practices in various businesses and industries.

### The National Archives

The second building from the top of the Federal Triangle, this is said to be the most beautiful archives building in the world.

At the front entrance on Constitution Avenue, a long flight of broad steps leads up to the massive doors. These are the largest doors on any structure in Washington: 49 feet high and 9 feet wide, and each door weighs 10 tons.

A huge sculptured figure is at either side of the steps, both here and at the entrance on Pennsylvania Avenue.

The inscription under the figure seated at the right of the entrance reads, "The Past is Prologue."

When the United States Government moved from Philadelphia to the new capital city, many important documents and valuable papers were stored in the Treasury Building, a frame structure near the President's Palace. The very next year, in 1801, the Treasury burned, although everyone turned out to help put out the fire; even President John Adams carried pails of water. Many irreplaceable records were destroyed in the flames. In 1810, Congress appropriated $20,000 for a fireproof depository, but no move was made toward building it.

By that time, governmental papers were being stored wherever there was room for them. Numerous documents were destroyed when the British burned the Capitol, the White House, the Treasury, and other buildings in 1814. Other important papers were lost in two disastrous Treasury fires in 1833 and 1877; but still the United States provided no safe place for its valuable records. Papers were not only burned but were also injured by dampness, insects, and mice and rats, and often many of them were stolen or lost. Many bundles of historic documents were once sold for junk by a careless clerk who knew nothing of their value. And, of course, dishonest autograph hunters and stamp collectors often helped themselves to many of the papers.

Finally, in 1926, Congress made an appropriation for a building in which all federal records and valuable papers were to be kept. It was to be a part of the great Federal Triangle, in the block between Pennsylvania and Constitution Avenues at Seventh Street. This was the site of the old Marsh Market, one of the swampiest, most rat-infested spots along the Mall, and there, too, old Tiber Creek rumbled along, deep underground. As this building was designed to last for centuries, and to be proof against fire and flood and absolutely uninhabitable by all destructive animals and insects, its construction was interesting and difficult.

As the first step, thousands of concrete piles were pushed down in the marshy ground for 30 or more feet, to form a firm foundation. On this base was built a huge, scow-shaped platform of concrete, at least 5 feet in thickness; in the center of this "mat" were installed two electric pumps and a powerful steam turbine. When the water in Tiber Creek reaches a certain level under this building, the first pump automatically goes to work, forcing the water into the Potomac River through a large pipe. If the water rises higher, a second pump kicks off and goes to work. And if the water reaches the floor stage, the big turbine, with its enormous pumping power, is quickly turned on.

The contents of this huge building are protected from every and any injury. The quality and quantity of air, the temperatures, the humidity are all carefully regulated. Even the bright sunlight is excluded. Before it is taken into the building, every bit of paper, each book and document is thoroughly fumigated and dusted so that even the hardiest little bookworm cannot survive.

Although the contents of the National Archives Building are for the most part documents and records of the Federal Government and war and pension records, they are not all just bundles of letters and papers and volumes of dry statistics. There are maps, photographs, motion pictures, sound recordings, and, among other things, several unusual treaties. But the most important of all the documents in the National Archives are the original copies of the Declaration of Independence, the Constitution, and the Bill of Rights—the most precious possessions of the United States.

The Constitution and the Declaration of Independence

had been on exhibition, under constant guard, on the second floor of the Main Building of the Library of Congress from February 28, 1924, until they were removed for transfer to their permanent home in the National Archives.

This excerpt from the report in the Library of Congress Information Bulletin tells of the careful procedure used in moving those rare, governmental documents.

"With the transfer of the Declaration of Independence and the Constitution of the United States to the National Archives on December 13, the April 30, 1952 directive of the Joint Committee of Congress on the Library, that these documents and other records of the Constitutional Convention be transferred for preservation in that institution, was complied with. The directive in turn complied with the Federal Records Act of 1950, which requires that all permanently valuable, noncurrent records of the Federal Government be preserved in the National Archives. The papers of the Continental Congress, the Articles of Confederation, and other records pertaining to the creation of the United States had been transferred previously. The transfer of the Declaration and the Constitution was delayed until Saturday in order that the National Archives could complete the preparation of its Shrine (which was part of the original structure of the Archives Building) for these documents and also for the record copy of the Bill of Rights. This latter document had already been in the possession of the National Archives but was recently placed in a helium-filled, thermopane enclosure similar to those in which the Declaration of Independence and the Constitution were enclosed last year. This was done in order to preserve the color of the ink used in the engraving of the documents. All three documents will be placed on permanent exhibition in the

The Washington Monument

The Lincoln Memorial

*Photo by Abbie Rowe—Courtesy National Park Service*

"In This Temple as in the Hearts of the People for Whom He Saved the Union, the Memory of Abraham Lincoln Is Enshrined Forever."

The Capitol

Puck surveys the Capitol dome from the Folger Library

The Jefferson Memorial

The White House

The White House after it was burned in the War of 1812

The Library of Congress and Annex. The Folger Library is at the left

The National Gallery of Art. The Mellon Memorial Fountain is in the foregro

Rotunda of the National Gallery of Art

The Supreme Court of the United States

The National Archives Building

The Pentagon

The Tomb of the Unknown Soldier, Arlington National Cemetery

*Photo by Abbie Rowe—Courtesy National Park Ser*

Mount Vernon

National Archives in a special dedicatory ceremony today, Bill of Rights Day."

Mr. Clapp, as Acting Librarian, and Senator Theodore Francis Green of Rhode Island, Chairman of the Joint Committee of Congress on the Library, officially turned the documents over to Brigadier General Stoyte O. Ross of the Air Force in a ceremony in the main hall of the Library shortly after 11 A.M. on December 13, 1952. The Department of Defense had arranged an impressive transfer ceremony providing for the security of the documents and symbolizing the devotion of the men and women in the Armed Services to the principles embodied in them. A special detail of 22 men from the Armed Services Police Detachment carried and guarded the documents as they were removed in their six helium-filled cases from the Library of Congress to an armored car, and from the armored car into the National Archives. Dr. Wayne C. Grover, Archivist of the United States, received the documents at the National Archives and accepted the responsibility for their custody in the future. The entire route of the procession from the Library of Congress to the National Archives was lined on both sides by a cordon of men and women of the four Armed Services. The Metropolitan Police Force of Washington provided a flying wedge of motorcycle police to head the procession. The Library of Congress Guard Force insured the safety of the documents until they were turned over to the representatives of the Defense Department.

### Department of Justice

Like all of the structures in the Federal Triangle, the Department of Justice Building is large and beautiful.

At the head of this department is the Attorney General

of the United States, a member of the Presidential Cabinet. The Attorney General and his numerous assistant attorneys general have charge of the legal affairs of our entire country.

*The Federal Bureau of Investigation.* There are many divisions and bureaus in the Department of Justice, but the one most popular and interesting, especially to boys and girls, is the Federal Bureau of Investigation, generally referred to as the FBI.

This bureau was established in 1908. Since 1924 it has grown rapidly in importance and usefulness to the United States Government. At that time, J. Edgar Hoover was appointed Director of the FBI. He at once began working to perfect an organization to fight crime and capture criminals.

Men between the ages of 25 and 40 years are carefully chosen and trained in a special school to learn all methods of detecting crime. They are taught the reading of fingerprints, photography, the methods of conducting an interview, and the use of firearms. Field divisions under the direction of these trained men are located in more than 50 cities in the United States.

In the FBI headquarters are technical laboratories where expert scientists examine and analyze bloodstains, bullets, bombs, casts of footprints, and everything that might furnish a clue to the crimes or criminals under investigation. Also in the possession of the FBI, although they are now found in another building, are more than 69,000,000 fingerprints filed on cards. These prints furnish positive identification of criminals and suspects, as no two persons in the world have fingerprints exactly alike.

In the exhibit cases are countless relics taken from notorious outlaws and "bad men." Their guns and other weapons are displayed. A tour through the FBI rooms is enlightening and thrilling.

FBI is the official abbreviation of this branch of the Department of Justice, but the term "G-man" was first used by a gangster. When "Machine Gun" Kelly was cornered and captured by the FBI agents, he cried, "Don't shoot, G-men, don't shoot!" The name stuck, and this abbreviation of "Government man" has become the common name of the FBI agents.

The initials FBI also have another meaning: On the seal of the Federal Bureau of Investigation are the words *Fidelity, Bravery, Integrity*.

### Internal Revenue Building

This is the fourth structure in the Federal Triangle, although it was the first to be completed, in 1930. It faces Constitution Avenue from Tenth to Twelfth Streets.

As the name indicates, the business conducted in this building is concerned with Federal taxes, and has no attraction for visitors.

### Post Office Department

An imposing building, this stands between Twelfth and Thirteenth Streets, facing Pennsylvania Avenue. It joins the arches of the Interstate Commerce Building which is directly behind it.

Both the interior and exterior of this building are elaborately decorated. On the outside, carved in bas-relief on the frieze across the façade, are the forms of communication: the smoke signals used by the American Indians, the carrier pigeons, the fire signals, and the modern postal system. Murals on the inner walls picture the history and progress of the United States mail service.

As this is the office of the Postmaster General, who is a member of the President's Cabinet, his suite of offices is spacious and elegant. Unusual statues portraying the United States postman through various periods, from 1691 to the present, decorate the Postmaster General's reception room.

Stamp collectors will be thrilled with the displays here. Specimens of every issue of United States postage stamps are in this exhibit, and many of them are for sale.

The street floor is occupied by a city post office, called the Twelfth Street Post Office or, sometimes, the Benjamin Franklin Post Office.

### Interstate Commerce Commission

This is the first of the three buildings extending from Twelfth to Fourteenth Streets. They appear as one great structure when viewed from the front on Constitution Avenue.

The Commission was created on February 4, 1887. Eleven men, appointed by the President, form this body. Among their duties are the regulation of the railroads, express companies, busses, steamship lines, and all carriers of passengers and freight, and the maintaining of reasonable rates and fares.

### Government Auditorium

This building is west of the Interstate Commerce Building and is joined to it by a colonnaded archway. A second, similar arch connects the Auditorium and the Labor Department on the opposite side.

### Department of Labor

Facing Constitution Avenue at the corner of Fourteenth Street is the home of the newest of the ten executive bodies in the Presidential Cabinet. It was not even suggested until after the Civil War, in 1865. A Bureau of Labor was set up under the Department of the Interior in 1884. A Department of Commerce and Labor was established in 1903, but it was not until 1913 that the independent Department of Labor was created.

The Secretary of Labor has charge of the welfare and the interests of all the wage-earners in the United States. Frances Perkins, the Secretary of Labor from 1933 to 1945, was the first woman to serve in a President's Cabinet.

### Department of Commerce

At the base of the Federal Triangle, at Fifteenth Street and Constitution Avenue, is the Department of Commerce Building. When it was completed, in 1932, it was the largest office building in Washington and one of the largest in the world.

The formation of this department of the Government dates back to one spring day in 1785 when a group of discouraged businessmen called on George Washington to ask for his help and advice. The Revolutionary War had been won, but the country's business was in a bad way. Tobacco and furs were the only exports, and there was little money in the new land. However, nothing came from the conference at that time.

On June 10, 1929, President Hoover laid the cornerstone of the new Department of Commerce Building, with the same silver trowel which President Washington has used at the laying of the Capitol cornerstone in 1793.

People were horrified at the great size of the building, and they were even more aghast at the cost. Seventeen and one-half million dollars for an office building! They protested loudly and named it "Hoover's Folly." But Mr.

Hoover paid no attention to the name or the protests; he had been Secretary of the Department of Commerce for two terms, and he knew all about it and its needs.

Old Tiber Creek still flows under all the buildings in the Federal Triangle; therefore, the Commerce Building, like the others, had to be constructed on a base of thousands of concrete pilings which would stretch 80 miles if they were laid end to end.

Broad corridors extend for five miles throughout these buildings, and 16 stairways and 36 elevators go from floor to floor. There are many bureaus, branches, and divisions in this far-reaching department of the Government which is concerned with travel over land, on the sea, and in the air. Charts and maps are made here for the guidance of airmen and navigators. Weather reports are constantly received from various places. One of the most important divisions of this department, the Bureau of Standards, has its own separate establishment almost four miles away, on Connecticut Avenue.

Two other important divisions of this department are the Patent Office and the Bureau of the Census. The Patent Office contains the drawings of all patents granted since 1790.

But the most interesting exhibit is that of the Bureau of Fisheries. The Department of Commerce superintends the care and conservation of fish in the waters of the United States, particularly the fish used for food and for various commercial purposes. The Aquarium is in the basement of this building and it is said that this basement is large enough to hold three great ocean liners, without crowding. The walls are lined solidly with large, upright glass tanks—48 of them—attractively decorated with water plants. And there, quite at home in their intriguing seascapes, are our American fish of all species, colors, and sizes. It is an interesting exhibit; you'd never believe such fish really exist. But there they are: gauzy-winged angel fish, hardy hellbenders, giant three-pound frogs, and an extensive collection of trout.

In the floor pools it is possible to have a close-up view of alligators and turtles of all sizes. A number of cases contain displays of various articles made from shells, fish scales, and coral, such as heads, buttons, and other ornamental novelties.

CHAPTER

**7**

# Around the Turn on Pennsylvania Avenue

## The Treasury Building

The Treasury Building brings Pennsylvania Avenue to an abrupt stop at Fifteenth Street. All traffic continuing on the avenue must turn north here for three blocks, where Pennsylvania Avenue again goes on its way west. Placing the Treasury Building at Fifteenth Street blocked the "magnificent vista" which L'Enfant had planned from the Capitol to the President's Palace.

President Andrew Jackson was responsible for this change. Robert Mills, the architect of the Treasury Building, was rather slow in starting the foundation. Jackson became impatient at the delay, and marched over from the President's Palace to see about the matter. Stamping across the lot to the east side, he thrust his cane down into the ground and announced loudly, "Here, right here, is where I want the cornerstone!" So President Jackson put the crook in Pennsylvania Avenue.

The Treasury of the United States is one of the three oldest governmental buildings in Washington; only the White House and the Capitol were erected earlier.

This is the third structure of this branch of the Government to be built on this site. The first Treasury, a wooden building of 30 rooms, was erected on the south end of the block. The British burned this in their invasion of the Capital, in 1814. A second frame building was built immediately, but it, too, was destroyed by fire, in 1833. Then Congress, realizing that this department of the Government required a permanent home for its increasing business, authorized a "fireproof building of such dimensions as may be needed for the present and for future accommodation."

The Treasury Building is one of the most notable examples of pure Greek architecture in the whole United States. Its 72 great Ionic columns, each made from a single piece of granite, form one of the outstanding colonnades in the world. Most of the granite used in this building was brought in sailing vessels from Maine, up the Potomac River to the Mall.

Although this building of 488 rooms seemed unnecessarily large when it was begun in 1836, the Treasury Department and its 25 bureaus and divisions have long since outgrown it. In 1919 the Treasury Annex was completed. It is the imposing building with the heavily grated windows, opposite the Treasury, just across Pennsylvania Avenue. This annex is connected with the main building by a tunnel under the surface of the street. And in addition 20 other buildings have wholly or partially been taken over for the use of the Treasury Department.

Besides having control of the Government's money, the Treasury is in charge of Customs, marine activities, the Bureau of Engraving and Printing, the Mints, and the United States Department of Secret Service. This latter section includes the White House Police Force which is entrusted with the protection of the President and his family, and also has charge of the suppression of counterfeiting. The Coast Guard is under the direction of the Treasury during peace-time, but is a department of the Navy when the country is at war.

The money vaults are under the Treasury, and below these vaults is a basement which facilitates frequent inspections, to prevent tunneling by robbers. Numbers of microphones have been installed to catch the slightest sound, and all locks automatically close when an alarm is sounded. The alarm also summons all guards, the city police, and a troop of cavalry from Fort Myer. There is, too, a supply of poison gas on hand to put any unwary burglar out of business.

### The White House

The white stone mansion at 1600 Pennsylvania Avenue has been pictured so often in its beautiful setting of fountains, flowers, and trees that it is familiar to all Americans, young and old. It has been the home of every President of the United States, with the exception of George Washington.

When he planned the city, Major L'Enfant selected 80 swampy acres for the "President's Palace and Park." George Washington chose the location for the house on the highest knoll in this area, which was about 40 feet above the level of the Potomac River.

Captain James Hoban won the prize of $500 offered by Congress for the design most suitable for the President's house. Charming in its dignified simplicity, it has remained in good style for more than a century and a half.

Three hundred years and one day after Columbus' discovery of America, on October 13, 1792, the cornerstone of the President's Palace was laid, with elaborate Masonic ceremonies. However, lack of money and labor difficulties delayed the progress of the building.

It was still far from completion when President John Adams and his wife arrived in November 1800, and it was in no sense a pretty picture at that time. Pigs, cows, geese, and other livestock roamed over the grounds wherever they chose. There were workmen's shanties, tool sheds, and piles of lumber and stones about the grounds, while rubbish and debris from the building littered the yard near the house. Dainty Mrs. Adams had to step over or around mud puddles in entering her new home.

Only six rooms were ready for occupancy, but Abigail Adams was an efficient woman and soon had cleared a room for the President's office. The East Room was unfinished. There was no furniture for it and no money to buy any; so it was used as a place in which to hang the household laundry to dry. So well did this Mrs. Adams manage affairs that she invited the public to a huge reception on New Year's Eve, not in the East Room, however; the party was held in the oval room on the second floor.

The President's Palace was burned when the British invaded Washington during the War of 1812. James Hoban rebuilt it according to his original plans, and the sandstone walls were painted white to hide the stains left by the flames and smoke. People began speaking of it as the "White House" at that time, and President Theodore Roosevelt made the name official in 1902.

The north and south porticoes and the wings at the east and west sides have been added through the years but, in the main, the simple lines of the building have been preserved. Early in World War II, an extension was added to the east wing and a large concrete air raid shelter was constructed underground, connected with the Treasury Building by a roomy tunnel.

There are six rooms on the ground floor of the White House. The famous East Room is used on great occasions: state receptions, weddings, funerals, and special religious services.

The oval Blue Room is thought by many to be the most beautiful in the mansion; this is the President's reception room. The woodwork and the mantel are white; the walls and the chairs are covered with blue brocade, and the windows are draped with the same material. The Red Room and the Green Room, named respectively for the color of their furnishings, are small reception rooms, identical in size. There is a private dining room besides the State Dining Room, which is very large and very formal. More than 100 guests can be seated at the horseshoe-shaped table at one time.

The second floor is occupied by the Presidential family. The oval room, above the Blue Room, is the President's library.

The third, or attic, floor contains 14 or more rooms used for extra bedrooms and storage and closet space. The large extensions on either side of the original house are executive and business offices. In the wing on the west are the executive offices, cabinet rooms, and quarters where the newspaper reporters and radio commentators gather. The President's aides and advisors have offices in the east wing, and many are housed in the old State Building west of the White House.

Throughout the years occasional changes and repairs have been necessary as different Presidents came into office. In 1889, when Benjamin Harrison moved into the White House, Mrs. Harrison, a fastidious housekeeper, disgusted at the hordes of rats infesting all parts of the house, urged Congress to build a new Executive Mansion on a different location. However, no attention was paid to this first lady's wishes.

President Theodore Roosevelt, in 1902, moved into a rented house while extra bedrooms and baths were installed on the third floor of the White House to accommodate his large family.

In March 1927, President Coolidge and his family moved into the home of Mrs. Eleanor Patterson on Dupont Circle while the White House was being re-roofed.

Harry S. Truman made plans for some extensive changes when he became President, but the Senate Appropriations Committee did not approve them. However, Mr. Truman succeeded in building the balcony he desired on the south portico, although that stirred up a great controversy. But in 1948 it was discovered that the noble old mansion was literally falling to pieces. The ceiling in the East Room was sagging and the floors of the second story were breaking through. Something had to be done. A few people favored the idea of building an entirely new structure but such strong opposition came from all quarters of the country that it was decided to repair the original building.

President Truman and his family moved across Pennsylvania Avenue to the Blair House which had been purchased in 1942 by the Government for a guest house. The Lee House, adjoining it, also had been bought by the Government in 1944, for the accommodation of additional guests. Connecting doors join the two houses to make roomier quarters for the Presidential household. A large conference room was provided in the old State Building for the President's press conferences.

In 1949, a bipartisan committee, appointed to manage the renovating of the White House, decided that the original outer walls of the mansion would be preserved. A new steel frame would be constructed inside the walls and a new and deep foundation would be built beneath them. Two extra levels were constructed underground to provide more storage space. Four large bedrooms, a recreation room, and an addition to the sky parlor were built on the top floor of the enlarged White House.

New decorating, draperies, and upholstery added to the splendor of the interior of the Executive Mansion. The East Room is dignified and stately, with walls and draperies of lemon, gold and white, instead of red and white as before. The Blue Room, Red Room, and Green Room were left in their original colors which were freshened up. The paneled walls of the State Dining Room were painted a soft blue-green. The family rooms on the second floor were all tastefully redecorated. In this work, Mrs. Truman, the first lady, assisted by expert decorators from New York, decided on the fabrics and colors to be used in the different rooms.

President Truman had the Presidential Seal raised from the floor of the main reception hall and hung it on the wall over the door of the Blue Room. He also had the eagle turned to face toward the emblem of peace—the olive branch—instead of away from it, and Mr. Truman then had the 13 stars on the seal increased to 48.

In 1951, the Queen of England, then Princess Elizabeth, with her husband, the Duke of Edinburgh, visited the United States. Arriving on October 31st, they and their party of nine were entertained by President and Mrs. Truman and their daughter Margaret at the Blair-Lee House. Toward the close of their visit, the visitors went with their hosts to the unfinished White House, and in the rose garden Princess Elizabeth presented the President with a gift from her father, King George VI. This was an antique overmantel, consisting of a rare pair of silver candelabra and a carved gilt mirror with an oil painting of flowers set above it.

President and Mrs. Truman took their royal guests on

a tour of the unfinished mansion, and called their attention to the Blue Room where it was planned to hang the overmantel. Later, however, this unusual gift was placed in the State Dining Room where it could be seen and admired by a greater number of people.

The Trumans moved back into the White House on March 28, 1952, after an absence of more than three years. The first royal guests entertained in the renovated Executive Mansion were Queen Juliana of the Netherlands and her husband, Prince Bernhard. They arrived April 3, 1952, on the royal airship, "The Flying Dutchman." Thousands of orange-colored tulips, from bulbs sent from Holland in honor of Juliana's royal family, bloomed around the great fountains on the south lawn and decorated many rooms in the White House.

Queen Juliana was publicly welcomed and presented with the key to the capital city by the District of Columbia Commissioners. This ceremony, as usual, took place on a flag-draped platform opposite the old District Building at Pennsylvania Avenue and Fourteenth Street.

There is one White House ceremony which is especially planned for Washington's younger citizens and visitors. This is the Easter Monday egg-rolling on the lawn of the Executive Mansion. The origin of this entertainment is uncertain, though some writers declare that Dolly Madison first started the custom. After dyeing great numbers of boiled eggs this friendly first lady is said to have invited the young children of her acquaintances to gather on the broad south lawn and roll the gay symbols of Easter down the long slope. Some authorities credit Andrew Jackson, the bachelor President James Buchanan, and President Hayes with initiating this hospitable gesture.

The egg-rolling has continued through the years, however, occasionally interrupted by tragic days of war. But on Easter Monday, April 6, 1953, after a lapse of 12 years, President and Mrs. Eisenhower revived the custom. Thousands of youngsters, girls and boys of all ages, dressed in their spring finery and carrying baskets of brightly colored eggs, flocked to the White House. Grown-ups were admitted only when accompanied by a child.

That the American people have a feeling of pride in the home of the Presidents is evident, but it is something deeper than pride. They have a sense of ownership in the home of the man who has been chosen to be the Chief Executive of their country. It is a sentiment not expressed in words, but in actions which seem involuntary; it is invariably displayed at a time of national crisis. Then people flock to the White House! Of course, some are there through curiosity, but not the majority.

When the tragic news of Pearl Harbor reached Washington, throngs gathered—instantaneously it seemed—around the White House. Wondering, angry men and women crowded close to the home of their leader. And on that April afternoon in 1945, in an inconceivably brief time after the word had come of the death of President Franklin D. Roosevelt, thousands, awed and grief-stricken, filled every foot of available space along Pennsylvania Avenue before the White House, and Lafayette Square across the street was crowded.

### The Ellipse

An oval park south of the White House, the Ellipse is officially a part of the White House grounds. It is used as a public playground or an athletic field. For many years this space was surrounded by a tall board fence painted white; for that reason, it was spoken of as "the white lot."

## Zero Milestone

An inconspicuous block of granite about 4 feet high stands a short distance off Seventeenth Street, on the north side of the Ellipse, directly across from the south lawn of the White House.

The name, Zero Milestone, is carved on the north side of the marker and also the insignia of the United States Army Motor Transport Corps. The inscription on the south side reads: "Point for Measurement of Distances from Washington on Highways of the United States." The east side states: "Starting Point of 2nd Transcontinental Motor Convoy over the Bankhead Highway, XIV-June-MCMXX." On the west side is inscribed: "Starting Point of 1st Transcontinental Motor Convoy over the Lincoln Highway, VII-July-MCMXIX."

According to the original map of the city, Major L'Enfant planned to erect such an "Itinerary Column" one mile east of the Capitol, from which all distances of places throughout the continent were to be calculated. This column was never built on the spot designated by L'Enfant, as the city grew toward the west instead of the east.

In 1920 Congress, realizing the necessity for such a column or marker for general information of tourists, authorized the erection of the Zero Milestone. It was decided to put it on the north side of the Ellipse on the meridian line of the District of Columbia, on which the White House stands.

## Lafayette Square

Washington's most popular park is located across "The Avenue," opposite the White House. This park, which at first was called "the President's Square," was made when

Pennsylvania Avenue was cut through. For years, this was just a trampled common; a number of huts were built there for the men working on the President's house and a public market occupied one side.

Then people began to build houses around the Square. Benjamin Tayloe built the first residence on the east side, one with attractive iron balconies. The home of Dolly Madison was on the northeast corner, just three doors from the Tayloes.

St. John's Episcopal Church, opposite Lafayette Park at Sixteenth and H Streets, was built in 1814.

In 1819 Commodore Stephen Decatur had architect Benjamin Latrobe build his fine brick house with the prize money that he had earned in the War of 1812 and in the battles with the pirates in the Mediterranean. The Decatur home is opposite the northwest corner of the Square. It and the three other houses just mentioned are still in use.

Decatur, fatally wounded by Commodore James Barron in a duel at Bladensburg, was carried, dying, to his home. All the neighbors hurried to give aid: the Reverend Dr. Hawley from St. John's, Dolly Madison, from across the Square, and the Monroes from the White House. Thousands of citizens gathered in the Square, just as people do today when anything important happens. For years after this tragedy the Decatur residence was called the "House of Blood."

For more than a century the President's Square was the center of fashionable society. Many famous personages, generals, diplomats, and statesmen, lived in the surrounding residences. After Lafayette's triumphal visit to the United States in 1824, his name was given to the square, and at about that time it was graded and enclosed with a picket fence. Twenty-five years later an iron fence supplanted the wooden one.

Near the center of the park is the statue of Andrew Jackson, the first equestrian statue erected in the United States. It was made from cannon captured by Jackson in the War of 1812. This statue has been severely criticized by artists, sculptors, and other authorities on art, who object to the position of the horse as unnatural and an impossible one for an animal to maintain. However, young Clark Mills, the sculptor, when commissioned by Congress to make the statue, bought a race horse and carefully trained him for more than a year to hold this pose. People who know Jackson's temperament declare that the pose of the steed would be most pleasing to him, for he was a fine horseman.

The statues at each corner of this famous square were erected in honor of the true and tried friends who came from foreign lands to aid America in her fight for independence. On the southeast corner is General Lafayette and a group of his fellow countrymen. On the southwest is the statue of Count Rochambeau, the commander of the French troops who came to help us in our battles for freedom. The Prussian general, Baron von Steuben, stands at the northwest corner of the square. He was the perfectionist drillmaster who reorganized and trained Washington's defeated army at Valley Forge. On the northeast corner is the statue of the handsome, dashing Thaddeus Kosciusko who came from Poland to serve as a general in the Revolutionary Army.

It is not its beauty but its human, friendly atmosphere which makes this old square so popular. It is always full of life; people old and young are there at all hours. Servicemen, with or without their sweethearts, lonely old men and women who enjoy feeding the flocks of eager pigeons, the tame gray squirrels, and even the greedy hordes of sparrows and starlings, gather daily in friendly Lafayette Square.

This is the nearest point from which to view the White House and the visitors who enter the well-guarded west gate, and perhaps to catch a chance glimpse of the President himself. From September 18, 1793, when the first great crowd of 1,500 persons met in the President's Square to march up to the top of Jenkin's Hill to see President Washington lay the cornerstone of the Capitol, to V-J Day, the evening of August 14, 1945, when thousands upon thousands of cheering, joyous people filled its every inch of space, Lafayette Park has ever been the meeting place of Washington people. It is still the center of Washington life where everyone in the capital city goes during times of national crisis.

### Blair House

Blair House is the second house west of Lafayette Square on Pennsylvania Avenue. There are two large brass tablets on the iron fence, one at each side of the entrance, giving the story of this lovely old residence.

Many distinguished Americans have visited at the Blair home. It was in this mansion that Robert E. Lee was offered the command of the Union Army, just before the War between the States. The members of the Blair family were the owners and principal occupants of the house until 1942, when the Government purchased it to be the official guest house of the United States.

During recent years many foreign dignitaries have been guests at Blair House, including King George of Greece, ex-King Peter of Yugoslavia, and the charming Princess Elizabeth and her husband, the Duke of Edinburgh. President Truman and his family resided here for most of the week after President Roosevelt's death, and again for a longer period during the renovation of the White House.

### Lee House

Lee House adjoins Blair House, and was bought by the Government in 1944 to be used as an additional guest house. In its architectural style and color—creamy white with green shutters—it harmonizes perfectly with the Blair mansion. When foreign guests occupy either the Blair or Lee House, their national flag is flown above it.

### United States Court of Claims

On the northwest corner of Pennsylvania Avenue and Seventeenth Street is one of the divisions of the Federal Court. The building was originally the Corcoran Art Gallery.

### The Weather Bureau

This governmental division is between Twenty-fourth and Twenty-fifth Streets, just a block north of Pennsylvania Avenue, where it is housed in the old Mexican Embassy.

In this Bureau are prepared weather forecasts, warnings, and bulletins for all branches of the Government, including the military, the Navy, air transport, agriculture, commerce, and shipping. The Weather Bureau exchanges reports with other nations and is closely connected with the Army, Navy, and airways. Weather reports and forecasts for the next 48 hours are sent regularly to ships at sea, lighthouses, aviators, farmers, railroad and transport agencies, forest rangers, builders, contractors, and cowboys.

Small balloons are released from instruments on the

roof of the building at regular intervals to observe the direction and the velocity of the upper air currents. The Weather Bureau receives information from its offices all over the country; it has its own printing plant and the publication of all weather data in the United States is supervised here.

Historic old Pennsylvania Avenue terminates shortly after it crosses the Rock Creek Bridge; it then merges into M Street at Twenty-ninth Street.

# 🏴 8 🏴

# *Important Buildings*

## *Corcoran Art Gallery*

This was the gift of W. W. Corcoran, a native of Washington who gave large sums of money to the city, to be used especially for cultural interests. Mr. Corcoran helped to plan the gallery and gave it to the city, with his entire art collection and an immense endowment to maintain the project.

This building differs from many of the modern structures in Washington since it has no columns and no eagles in its exterior decoration. Instead, high on the roof, two fierce-looking griffins stand guard, one at the extreme south and the other at the north end of the gallery. This is, of course, an appropriate place for such decoration, for the mythological griffins were known as the special guardians of treasure, and there are countless treasures in the Corcoran Gallery. On either side of the entrance are bronze lions, copied from those by Canova at the tomb of Pope Clement XIII in St. Peter's in Rome.

Mr. Corcoran always aimed to foster American art and

to encourage American artists. He established a free art school in the gallery which enrolls approximately 500 students annually. The Corcoran Gallery is now considered one of the greatest in the United States.

### American Red Cross

This important organization occupies the four buildings one block south of the Corcoran Art Gallery on Seventeenth Street. Our American Red Cross Society was organized in 1881 by Clara Barton whose home was at Glen Echo, just a short distance from Georgetown. During the Civil War, Miss Barton had headed the war relief work, and later she was in charge of the work of the Red Cross. Clara Barton was the president of this society for 32 years.

The huge Headquarters Building, with the brilliant red cross gleaming high on its white marble wall, was built as a memorial to the brave women of the Civil War. It is dedicated to Mercy. In this main building are the offices of the National Headquarters' personnel, and a library and museum are in the basement.

The north building on E Street was opened in 1929 as a memorial to the women of World War I. The Ionic columns on this north front were gifts and are inscribed with the names of the donors and of the persons memorialized. On the second floor there is a large auditorium.

The third building, facing Eighteenth Street, is strictly an office building, opened in 1929 as an annex to the National Headquarters Building. The three periodicals, "The Red Cross Courier," the "Junior Red Cross Journal," and the "Junior Red Cross News," are published in this annex. The fourth building, completed in January, 1953, houses the District of Columbia Chapter of the Red Cross.

The courtyard formed by the three buildings is artistically landscaped around a bronze statue, dedicated to the memory of Jane Delano and 296 other brave nurses who died in World War I.

### D.A.R. Buildings

Three great marble buildings, filling an entire city block, make up this group belonging to the Daughters of the American Revolution. The buildings were financed by women's voluntary contributions.

The cornerstone of the first of these buildings, Continental Memorial Hall, was laid on the anniversary of the Battle of Lexington, April 19, 1904. It is a magnificent building of white Vermont marble. The auditorium is a copy of an old New England town meeting hall, and here the flag made by Betsy Ross hangs from the ceiling, and Peale's "porthole" portrait of George Washington adorns the wall. These are two treasures that no money can buy. In the exhibit rooms on either side of the hall are many priceless antiques.

Needing more space, the society built Administration Hall in 1923. Constitution Hall was erected in 1929, and is connected with the administration building. This great hall contains the auditorium and library; the auditorium seats 4,000 persons and it has the best acoustics of any building in the city. On the second floor is the extensive D.A.R. library, consisting mainly of American historical works and records.

### Pan-American Building

This is considered by many persons to be the most beautiful building in Washington. The statuary group on the north side of the entrance represents Washington bidding farewell to his generals; and South America is symbolized, on the opposite side, by the meeting of San Martin and Simon Bolivar. At the top of each pillar are, respectively, the emblems of North and South America—the eagle and the condor.

The patio, with its tropical plants and birds and the unusual fountain, is distinctly Latin American in design and feeling. In a large exhibit room are carved cabinets, chairs, and chests of beautiful wood. Cases around the walls contain displays of butterflies, brilliant birds, precious stones, and the products of each country represented, while colored dioramas provide interesting views of the other Americas. On either side of the entrance hall, broad stairways of black and white marble lead to the second floor where the "Hall of the Americas," the gallery of flags and heroes, and the richly decorated board room are the outstanding features. An immense library is available to those doing research on the member countries and related subjects.

The large doors of the exhibit room open on a broad terrace which overlooks a formal, blue-flowered garden bordering a large pool lined with bright blue tiles. A statue of Xochipillo, known as the "sad Indian," the god of flowers in Aztec mythology, is seated on the edge of the pool against a background of the blue-tiled walls of the loggia. A more serene and peaceful spot cannot be imagined.

All the Americas—the 21 republics of North and South America—sent delegates to a conference in Washington in 1889. They formed a Union for the promotion of friendship, peace, and trade—an idea which Henry Clay and John Quincy Adams had strongly advocated 70 years earlier.

This organization was called the Pan-American Union, and from the beginning the 21 republics have all shared in the expenses. The United States bought the block at the corner of Seventeenth Street and Constitution Avenue for $200,000, and donated it for the site of the buildings. Andrew Carnegie, who was a delegate to the conference, gave $900,000 toward the building, and the remaining necessary sum was contributed by the various republics. Around the corner, west on Constitution Avenue, is a large and attractive building, only recently completed; here are the offices of the staff administering the affairs of the Pan-American Union.

### Department of the Interior

The Interior Department Building covers two square blocks, more than 5 acres. When it was completed, this was the largest air-conditioned office building in the world.

The idea of this department of the Government originated with Thomas Jefferson in 1784. But no organization was formed until the necessity for a special department to attend to the opening of public lands to settlers led to the establishment of the "Home Department," as it was first called, in 1849. Today the Department of the Interior controls a vast number of important bureaus and divisions concerned with the welfare of the country and the people.

### The Octagon House

On the corner of Eighteenth Street and New York Avenue is an unusual building. It is one of Washington's oldest residences, and its story is closely associated with at least one historic event.

Colonel John Tayloe, a wealthy Virginia planter planned to build a winter home in Philadelphia; but George Washington, his close friend, persuaded him to build in the capital city. Washington himself chose the lot, which sold for $1,000. Dr. William Thornton, the designer of the Capitol, drew the plans for this unique house which was completed in 1800. The bricks, mantels, and most of the materials and furnishings came from England.

The hospitable Tayloes entertained Washington society and many prominent foreign guests in their stately home, but the Ocatagon House reached the high point of its existence after the burning of the President's Palace, in the War of 1812. Colonel Tayloe, then at his country estate in Virginia, offered the Octagon House to President Madison for his residence until the Executive Mansion was restored. Here the President signed the Treaty of Peace with Great Britain at the very table now in that circular room on the second floor.

A fine curved stairway leads down into the large hall and the circular vestibule; there, in the niches originally made for them, are two wood-burning iron stoves. Secret doors lead from the hall and the dining room to the back stairs and down to a hidden entrance to a tunnel, or really two tunnels—one leading to the President's House and the other to the river; it is said that boats were once anchored on the Potomac near the outlet of the tunnel. The original stables, the cook house, and the slave quarters are at the rear of the garden.

The American Institute of Architects considered the Octagon House one of the finest examples of early American architecture, and in 1902 they bought it from the Tayloe heirs for their national headquarters.

### Girl Scouts' Little House

This small, vine-covered cottage, on the southeast corner of New York Avenue and Eighteenth Streets, is the property of the Girl Scouts of America, and is an example of the quaint New England, "salt box" type of architecture. It is a reproduction of the house of John Howard Payne, the author of "Home Sweet Home."

Mrs. Herbert Hoover, when she was the honorary president of the National Girl Scouts, purchased the house and presented it to the organization.

## Public Health Service

Four beautiful white marble buildings lie between Nineteenth and Twentieth Streets on the north side of Constitution Avenue. The first in order was erected in 1933 for the administration offices of the Public Health Service.

During World War II this building was assigned to the War Department. At present it is occupied by the Atomic Energy Commission.

## The Federal Reserve Board

The second of this group of outstanding buildings, the Federal Reserve Board Building, is one of the most admired of all the newer structures in Washington. The simplicity of its white marble exterior is relieved only by the wrought iron balustrades at either side. The magnificent black marble fountains at each front corner of the lawn are strikingly effective. This building is devoted to the management of the Federal Reserve Banks, national and other general banking interests.

## National Academy of Sciences

The National Academy of Sciences, the third in this quartet of beautiful buildings, is not strictly a governmental agency; it is listed as a quasi official agency and it owns its own building.

This agency was organized during the Civil War when 50 of the country's leading scientists were asked to undertake some necessary research for the Government. Later this agency developed into the National Academy of Sciences, established by an Act of Congress. The Act specifies that ". . . the Academy shall, whenever called upon by any department of the Government, investigate, examine, experiment and report upon any subject of science or art, the actual expense of such investigations, examinations, experiments and reports to be paid from appropriations which may be made for the purpose, but the Academy shall receive no compensation whatever for any services to the Government of the United States." This Act was approved by President Lincoln in 1863.

The building and an endowment for its maintenance were made possible by a gift of $5,000,000 from the Carnegie Corporation in 1919. Many interesting demonstrations of scientific experiments and of natural phenomena are exhibited to the visiting public.

### American Institute of Pharmacy

The fourth and last building in this row, like its neighbor, is not a Government-owned building. It is the headquarters of the druggists of the United States. The American Pharmaceutical Association erected it with funds contributed by their members and other interested individuals. The American Institute of Pharmacy is not a governmental bureau, but it may be considered an official governmental aide. All lists of drugs, prescriptions, and formulas which should be found in every drug stock are supervised by members of this body.

A ring of the doorbell will admit visitors to this small and picturesque building where there are a number of interesting things to see. A life-sized bronze statue of William Proctor, Jr., the Father of Pharmacy, occupies a prominent place in the foyer, while on the right are the library and reference room. Opening from the left of the foyer is a museum containing rare antique bottles, scales, mortars and pestles, and recipes and prescriptions that are centuries old.

CHAPTER

 9

## Potomac Park

Potomac Park extends from Constitution Avenue to the tip of Hains Point. It was for many years Washington's most popular playground; golf, baseball, football, polo, miniature golf, horseback riding, bicycling, boating, and fishing were all enjoyed in these grounds. But since the beginning of World War II, much of this space has been used for offices and dormitories for service women, and there is less room for sports.

In the early days of the capital city the area west of the Washington Monument down to the Potomac River was a stretch of useless swamp. It was called the Potomac Tidal Flats and was said to be good only to breed the mosquitoes which caused malaria.

In 1901 the McMillan Park Commission made plans to fill in this marsh and extend the Mall to the river's edge. By this means more than 390 acres of land were reclaimed with a waterfront of $3\frac{5}{8}$ miles.

Potomac Park was Mrs. William Howard Taft's pet project. She had visions of making it an attractive park similar to the beautiful Luneta in Manila, which she had admired when President Taft had been the Governor of the Philippines. Mrs. Taft promoted the building of a fine bandstand, a short distance south of the Washington Monument, and arranged for Wednesday and Saturday concerts by the Marine Band.

## Water Gate

In the recreational area northwest of the Lincoln Memorial is a broad flight of granite steps leading from the plaza down to the platform at the river's edge. It is used to seat the vast audiences at the Water Gate concerts. The stage is built on a barge, anchored just off the shore in front of the steps; and there the National Symphony Orchestra, operatic companies, and other musical organizations present programs throughout the summer months.

Water Gate was originally intended for the reception of any high officials or celebrities arriving at the capital by water, or for any official Naval affairs.

## Riverside Drive

Riverside Drive begins near the Ericsson Monument, south of the Lincoln Memorial, and encircles Potomac Park. The Potomac shore is lined with graceful weeping willow trees which are said to be the descendants of the willows around the tomb of Napoleon at St. Helena. Admiral Porter was the representative of the United States when Napoleon's body was removed from St. Helena to Paris. The admiral admired the willows near the Emperor's grave and brought a strong young sapling home with him to Washington. Many cuttings were made from this historic tree, and from these came our beautiful willows. These trees are especially effective where they border the sea wall on the two sides of this long peninsula.

## The Cherry Blossoms

The cherry blossoms are Riverside Drive's greatest attraction in the springtime, and Washington owes its famous cherry trees to Mrs. William Howard Taft.

When Taft was President, the United States was on friendly terms with Japan. The Viscountess Chinda, the wife of the Japanese Ambassador, knew that Mrs. Taft wished to plant some of the Japanese trees in Potomac Park. She asked her friend, Madame Osaki, the wife of the Mayor of Tokyo, to send her some small cherry trees. The Viscountess didn't know that these trees had never been allowed to grow outside of the Imperial Gardens in Tokyo. But the Mayor, eager to oblige, sent 3,000 young trees. Upon their arrival in America it was discovered that they were all infected by a destructive parasite, and there was nothing to do but destroy the whole shipment.

When Mayor Osaki heard of it, he had cuttings taken from the trees in the Mikado's own garden and planted them in chemically prepared soil, in insect-proofed nurseries. When the trees were large enough, he sent 3,020 of them in the charge of a whole staff of Japanese entomologists to Mrs. Taft in America.

The park gardeners had been ordered to plant elm trees around the Tidal Basin, but Mrs. Taft knew that here was the perfect setting for those cherry trees. The President's wife had her way, and she it was who planted the first tree and Viscountess Chinda the second. They are marked with metal plates and are several hundred yards west of the John Paul Jones Monument at the south end of Seventeenth Street, Northwest. These are the pale pink, single, early-blooming trees, blossoming between March 20th and April 15th.

Farther down on the left are the deep pink, double-flowered, oriental cherry trees which bloom several weeks later than the single variety. Quantities of these trees border the drive and groups of them are dotted over the adjoining golf course. In the early spring the shore of the Tidal Basin is a picture out of fairyland. Thousands and thousands of people journey from far and wide to see the beautiful blossoms.

### The Tidal Basin

This is actually a flush basin to clear out the accumulations in the harbor at low tide. Without this the Washington Channel with no outlet was like a dead-end street. Flood gates were placed at either end of this new body of water. At high tide the Potomac River gate is opened, and the channel gate is closed. The water backs up and fills the basin. At low tide the river gate is closed, the channel gate is opened, and the surplus water flows out of the basin under the Fourteenth Street bridge and sweeps out the channel. Small pleasure boats find the Tidal Basin an excellent boating place.

There is usually good fishing in the Potomac River and in Washington Channel around Potomac Park, and many a Washington fisherman likes to enjoy the sport with as little exertion as possible. He uses several lines—sometimes as many as three or four—each on the end of a pole or stick. Tying a little bell on the line, 6 or more inches from the end of the pole, he throws the baited hook over the railing into the water, pushes the other end of the pole firmly down into the ground, and relaxes on a nearby bench, or stretches out on the grass for a nap. When a fish nibbles the bait, the bell tinkles; the fisherman answers the summons, and hauls in his catch.

### Fort Leslie J. McNair, the National War College

This group of buildings can be seen across the channel as we continue up the Drive. It is located on a long rectangular peninsula where the Anacostia River and the Washington Channel join the Potomac. Here is offered the highest training in military postgraduate courses given in any Army War College in the United States. It is one of the oldest army posts in the country. When it was first established, in 1797, it was called Fort Humphrey.

In 1804 it was renamed Greenleaf's Point, and the first arsenal was built there. During the Civil War it became a military prison and the assassins of President Lincoln, including Mrs. Surratt, were hanged in the prison yard and buried under their cells.

### Bolling Field

On the east side of the Anacostia River, opposite the National Airport, across from Hains Point and Fort Leslie J. McNair, is this well guarded air base of 935 acres. It is used jointly by the Army Air Corps and the Navy Air Force.

### Washington Channel

The channel is a busy harbor for boats of all sorts and sizes, spacious launches, trim yachts, sail boats, and motor boats. There at the docks are the passenger boats—the *Potomac,* the *Robert E. Lee,* and others—ready to take sightseers to view Mount Vernon, travelers to Norfolk, or merrymakers on a moonlight cruise. In the early morning the wharf is crowded with oyster boats, boats filled with fish, as well as farm produce and fruits from Maryland and Virginia farms.

This is Washington's one fish market, and for several blocks along the adjoining streets all varieties of sea food are displayed. Markets of all kinds follow, for this is the district of the commission houses.

## The Jefferson Memorial

This classic, columned structure of white Vermont marble is beautifully situated at the north end of the Tidal Basin. The memorial is designed in the Roman Pantheon style of architecture which Thomas Jefferson had always admired. It is especially attractive in the early spring, when the blossoming cherry trees surround it like fluffy pink clouds. Many of the shrubs and trees beautifying the grounds about the memorial were brought from Jefferson's own home, Monticello.

The circular interior, the rotunda, is 80 feet in diameter and is lined with Georgia marble. On the paneled walls are inscriptions from Jefferson's writings. On the first are phrases from the Declaration of Independence; on the second panel is inscribed his doctrine of Freedom of Mind, based on his Virginia statute for religious freedom. The third panel bears his concepts of freedom of body and his belief in educating the people; the fourth contains Jefferson's ideas on government.

In the center of this rotunda the statue of Jefferson, 18 feet tall, is mounted on a pedestal 7 feet high. It is modeled from the full-length, front-view portrait painted by the American artist, Thomas Sully, during Jefferson's Presidency. The tall, lean figure wears a long, fur-lined coat, knee breeches, and buckled shoes, and holds a roll of papers in his left hand. The statue and inscriptions in bronze are in effective contrast to the creamy marble walls. A sculptured group on the pediment above the center front shows Jefferson, Franklin, John Adams, Roger Sherman, and Robert Livingston, the committee appointed to frame the Declaration of Independence.

One hundred sculptors entered designs for the Jefferson statue. The plan submitted by Rudolph Evans, a native of Virginia, was awarded the $35,000 prize.

The Jefferson Memorial was dedicated on the two-hundredth anniversary of Jefferson's birth, April 13, 1943. This was during World War II, and armed troops patrolled the grounds and surrounded the monument. A colorful addition to the scene was the presence of the Monticello Guards, one of the oldest military organizations in the country, and one to which Jefferson himself had belonged. The Guards were dressed in copies of the original gay Colonial uniforms of red, white, blue, and buff, topped by jaunty cocked hats.

President Franklin D. Roosevelt gave the dedicatory address; Grace Moore, the popular Metropolitan Opera star, sang "The Star-Spangled Banner," and the Marine Band played. An interesting feature of the program was the placing of the original Declaration of Independence in full view at the foot of the statue of its author. This famous document, framed in a 400-pound metal tablet, all safely enclosed in bullet-proof glass, was carried to the Memorial from the Congressional Library by a detail of Marines. Few of the spectators were aware that this was the original copy of the Declaration of Independence. This precious document had been secretly conveyed from its wartime hiding place in the bullion room of the United States Depository at Fort Knox, Kentucky, especially for this occasion. It remained in its position at the Jefferson Memorial for a week, constantly under heavy guard. It was viewed there by thousands of patriotic Americans, eager to see the document which has been called "the Birth Certificate of the United States of America."

The Jefferson Memorial completed L'Enfant's original plan for five grand points in the central area of the capital.

Here, at the very heart of the capital city, are the two oldest government buildings: The White House, the home of the President, and the Capitol, the home of the United States Government. And here, too, are the memorials honoring our three greatest men: Washington, who won our freedom from British rule; Lincoln, who preserved our Union; and Jefferson, who wrote our Declaration of Independence.

# 🎌 10 🎌

## Down Capitol Hill

### Union Station

Washington's only passenger terminal for all railroads entering the capital is at the foot of a broad, grassy slope north of the Senate Office Building.

The McMillan Commission chose this site of 25 acres, and the United States Government, the District of Columbia, and the railroads all shared the cost of the building and the grounds. The Union Station, completed in 1908, was the first building erected under the direction of the new commissioners. Daniel Burnham, the Chairman of the Board, planned it and made it a model for other builders to follow in beautifying Washington.

Built of white Vermont marble, in the Roman style of architecture, it combines beauty and utility. In order to accommodate the enormous crowds attending the Presidential inaugurations and other celebrations in the capital, this railroad station was built on a huge scale. It is said that the great concourse alone will hold 50,000 people.

Above the high arched entrance are granite statues, 18 feet in height, symbolizing Fire, Electricity, Agriculture,

Mechanics, Freedom, and Imagination, each with an appropriate inscription. Directly in front, in a wide circular plaza, is Lorado Taft's Columbus Memorial fountain, which shows the discoverer of America standing at the prow of his ship, gazing toward the new world.

Visitors coming to Washington see, along the incline to the Capitol, an immense fountain with glittering sheets of water and a large reflecting pool. This makes a gorgeous picture, especially at night when the sprays of water gleam in colored lights, and the illuminated dome of the Capitol is viewed across the plaza. Beneath this hillside is an underground garage for the use of the occupants of the Senate Office Building. There is also a tunnel for the street cars and farther down, on a lower level, the railroads enter the Union Station, thus leaving an unobstructed view to the Capitol, half a mile away.

### The City Post Office

The Post Office faces Massachusetts Avenue between North Capitol and First Streets, Northeast. Every practical convenience for conserving the time and effort of the employees has been installed in this building. Conveyor belts carry the mail from one part to another in the building; bucket lifts take loads from floor to floor, and a regular little trolley transports mail from room to room. An enclosed bridge over First Street connects the Post Office with the Union Station. There is also an underground tunnel through which the conveyor belts bring the mail directly from the trains to the Post Office.

Engraved on the exterior east and west cornices are the following appropriate lines:

> Messenger of sympathy and love
> Servant of parted friends
> Consoler of the lonely

Bond of the scattered family
Enlarger of the common life

Carrier of news and knowledge
Instrument of trade and industry
Promotor of mutual acquaintance,
Of peace, and of good will
Among men and nations.

### Government Printing Office

Washington's noisiest office, the Printing Office, is diagonally across North Capitol Street from the Post Office, and is the largest, best equipped printing office in the world. It is the United States' own printing establishment, where Government documents are planned, printed, and bound. Every sort of governmental printed matter, from a two-penny postal card to a technical, illustrated scientific work, is produced here. Everything used in the processes of printing and binding will be found here in huge quantities: great tubs or vats of varicolored ink, giant kettles of strong-smelling glue, and tons and tons of paper.

Perhaps the most important job of the Government Printing Office is the printing of the daily proceedings of Congress. No matter how late the Senate and the House remain in session, the stenographic copy of every speech or debate is rushed to the Government Printing Office, where it is immediately transcribed, printed, and bound. It is then put into an underground conveyor and shot to the Post Office across the street, in time to reach each senator and representative early the following morning.

### Municipal Center

North of the Avenue, between Third and Sixth Streets, a few blocks below the Capitol, is an area called Judiciary Square. These four squares eventually are to be wholly devoted to a group of City and District buildings to be known as the Municipal Center. Already there are several structures in this space.

The *District Administration Building* is at the northeast corner between C and D Streets. The *Public Library,* the new administration building, has been built at the southwest corner of this area. It is now occupied by the executive offices of the Public Library staff. The *United States Court House,* at the southeast corner, was completed in 1952.

The *Court House of the District of Columbia,* one of the oldest buildings in Washington, is located across Indiana Avenue, facing south toward Pennsylvania Avenue. It is much admired as one of the finest examples of the Greek architectural style in the city, but now, having become outgrown, it will be replaced.

The *Lincoln Statue,* facing south in front of the Court House, was the first monument erected in honor of Abraham Lincoln. It was paid for by public subscription and unveiled on the third anniversary of Lincoln's death.

The *District Court of Appeals,* the *District of Columbia Juvenile Court,* the *Police Court,* and the *Municipal Court* are all in this area called Judiciary Square. They are built in the same style and of the same material as those of the District Court House.

### The Lincoln Museum

Originally Ford's Theater, this museum is located on the east side of Tenth Street between E and F Streets. It was first used as a Baptist church. In 1862, J. T. Ford, a theatrical producer, bought it and made it into a fine theater. It was destroyed by fire a year later, and immediately Mr. Ford replaced it with a larger, finer building.

This was Washington's most popular playhouse and it was acknowledged to be one of the best equipped theaters in the United States.

On the night of April 14, 1865, it was the scene of the assassination of President Lincoln and was never again used as a theater. President and Mrs. Lincoln, with their two guests, Major Henry Rathbone and his fiancée, Miss Harris, occupied an upper box at the theater. Near the end of the play, John Wilkes Booth, acting on a carefully made plan, entered the box and shot the President, fatally wounding him. Major Rathbone seized the murderer, but Booth stabbed him with a dagger and leaped from the box. As he jumped, his spur became entangled in one of the flags draped on the railing of the box, causing him to fall on the stage and break his ankle. Nevertheless, Booth escaped, but he was captured 12 days later.

The President was carried across the street to the small, unpretentious home of a tailor, William Peterson. There, in a little front bedroom on the first floor, very plain and simply furnished, President Lincoln died at 7:22 the following morning, April 15, 1865.

Secretary Stanton took over the theater and cancelled all the performances, but returned it to the owner in June. However, when it became known that Ford intended to reopen the theater, the public would not allow it, and the Government was forced to forbid its use for that purpose. When the owner threatened to sue for his rights, the Government bought the building and the War Department used it for years. In 1932 the first floor was opened as a Lincoln museum. There are many articles here connected with the actual tragedy—Booth's gun and spur, the flag which draped the Presidential box—as well as exhibits from Lincoln's home and others generally related to his times and life.

The Government also purchased the Peterson house

where Lincoln died. It has been left exactly as it was on the day of his death, and it also is open to the public.

## Massachusetts Avenue

This is the longest street in Washington, extending from the Anacostia River northwest 10½ miles. It is a thoroughfare of contrasts—passing from the old District Jail through rows of shabby apartments and old houses and large marble buildings, such as the City Post Office and the Union Station, until it enters the aristocratic northwest section of the city. On this part of the avenue are the residences of prominent people as well as the many foreign legation and embassy buildings. Directly opposite many of these is an extensive wooded area, a surprising sight in the midst of a large city.

*The Luther Place Memorial Church,* between Fourteenth Street and Vermont Avenue, Northwest, was built a few years after the Civil War as a memorial of thanksgiving for national peace and unity.

*The Mount Vernon Methodist Church.* The largest Methodist Church in the capital, this is across from the Public Library at 900 Massachusetts Avenue.

*The Main Public Library.* The library was the gift of Andrew Carnegie in 1903, and extends from Seventh to Ninth Streets, Northwest, at Mount Vernon Square. When the new building in Municipal Center is completed, this will become a branch library.

*"A House That a Book Built."* At 1770 Massachusetts Avenue, Northwest, is the former home of Mrs. Frances Hodgson Burnett, the successful writer, built with the proceeds from her famous book, "Little Lord Fauntleroy."

*Phillips Memorial Art Gallery.* In 1918 Mr. Duncan Phillips, an art lover and critic, gave his home and fine art collection to the city in memory of his mother, father, and brother. The building is on Twenty-first Street, just off Massachusetts Avenue. Many works of the old masters are on exhibit here as well as those of modern artists. Frequent concerts and recitals by outstanding musicians are held in the Phillips Gallery.

*The First Mosque in America.* At Massachusetts Avenue and Belmont Road is an unusual building. It is a Moslem temple, the only such place of worship in the whole Western Hemisphere. It was constructed by the Washington Mosque Foundation, Incorporated, and this organization is sponsored by all the Moslem countries: Pakistan, Iraq, Persia, Afghanistan, Saudi-Arabia, Syria, and Egypt.

The mosque was begun in 1949. It is built of creamy Alabama limestone and topped by a tower more than 150 feet in height. From a balcony on the tower a man chants daily at the appointed hours for prayer. (The orthodox Moslems pray five times a day: morning, noon, afternoon, sunset, and night.) The mosque is placed at a slight angle from Massachusetts Avenue, as the building must face Mecca. All Moslems, when they pray, must face east in the direction of Mecca, the birthplace of Mohammed and the center of the Islamic faith.

The front of the mosque opens into a patio with a fountain in the center to supply the water necessary in the regular ritual of washing, as no Moslem ever enters the presence of God unclean. The mosque contains no sculpture or pictures. The Koran, which is the Moslem Bible, forbids the representation of any living beings in their places of worship. Geometric designs and selections from the Koran decorate the walls.

There are no pews or seats as the congregation sits on the floor which is covered with rich, vividly colored carpets and rugs. A magnificent chandelier adds to the beauty of the temple.

*Naval Observatory.* The observatory is on the second highest point in Washington, at Massachusetts Avenue and Thirty-fourth Street, Northwest. This institution furnishes an important service to people all over the world —on land and sea. The principal function of the observatory is the collection of the accurate data for naval astronomy and the recording and broadcasting of the standard time.

Although the United States Naval Observatory now ranks as one of the greatest in the world, it was many years in the making. Congress could not be made to see the importance of an observatory. As early as 1809, William Lambert, an amateur astronomer, figured the longitude of the Capitol in Washington and suggested that Congress should establish a first meridian in the United States. But the Congressmen, not realizing the value of the suggestion, and having no money to waste on theories, pigeonholed the papers and ignored the request.

In 1812, James Monroe, Secretary of State, wrote Congress, "An observatory would be of essential utility." John Quincy Adams was so enthusiastic about the project that people joked about "Mr. Adams and his lighthouse in the sky."

After much prodding, Congress put the matter in the hands of a special committee. To their astonishment they found that during the presidency of Thomas Jefferson all the requisite books and instruments for a naval observatory had been procured, and those—with an estimate of the cost of establishing it, and a survey of the coast—had been stored away in the War Department since that time.

In 1830, the Secretary of the Navy ordered the establishment of a depot of charts and instruments where chronometers, theodolites, and other equipment might be stored and tested before being issued to the Navy. It was first located in a small circular building on G Street, between Seventeenth and Eighteenth Streets, Northwest. In 1840, the first time signal was used in Washington. This was the time ball—a metal ball dropped from the top of a tall pole on a high building on the stroke of twelve, noon. This pole was usually placed on the roof of a tall building where it would be visible to ships in the harbor. Mariners peered through their spyglasses to see the time ball drop, and so they obtained the correct time for their chronometers. In 1885 the time ball was atop the State War and Navy Building. But it is necessary for an observatory to have an unobscured view of the sky, also to be protected from the glare of lights and the noise and vibrations of street traffic. For those reasons, in 1893 this department of the Navy was established on a 72 acre tract of land at the top of the hill on Massachusetts Avenue. The Observatory and 21 other buildings belonging to it now occupy this site; many are small, one-room houses erected simply to house delicate instruments.

In the exact center of a 1,000-foot circle, deep down in underground vaults, are three clocks. They are sealed airtight to remain unaffected by vibrations, change of temperature, and air pressure. Through a periscope mounted over the vault, the clocks may be checked without entering the vault itself. Time signals are flashed by radio every hour from these clocks. They establish standard time for the United States, navigators at sea, surveyors, engineers, scientific workers, and commercial laboratories.

The Naval Observatory also publishes a nautical almanac containing information about the tides, the location of certain stars on different dates, and other facts important to navigators.

*Washington Cathedral.* The Episcopal cathedral is on Mount St. Alban, the highest point in the city, 400 feet above the level of the Potomac. Popularly known as the

Washington Cathedral and sometimes as the National Cathedral, its official name is the Cathedral of St. Peter and St. Paul. Although Congress granted the charter for this huge church in 1893, not until 1907 was the cornerstone laid. By 1938 $12,000,000 had been spent, but the Cathedral is still unfinished and will not be completed for many years.

Built in the fourteenth century Gothic style of architecture and resembling England's cathedrals, it will be one of the ten largest churches in the world. There will be standing room for 27,000 people and seats for as many as 8,000. The grounds of the cathedral extend over 67 acres.

Conforming to the custom of Westminster Abbey, the tombs of many of America's famous people are in the cathedral. Woodrow Wilson, the twenty-eighth President of the United States, is buried here and above his tomb are three historic flags: the two Presidential flags presented to him at his two inaugurations, in 1913 and 1917, and the flag carried by the first American troops to march through London during World War I.

There are 35 chapels in the cathedral, including the exquisitely beautiful Children's Chapel. This in one of two cathedral chapels for children. The whole interior of the huge edifice is richly decorated and contains many rare items of historic interest. The cornerstone was brought from Bethlehem in Judea, and in the high altar are twelve stones from Solomon's quarry in Jerusalem.

Artistic plantings surround the various buildings in the grounds—the College of Preachers, the National Cathedral School for Girls, and the Boys' School. Near this last building is the Glastonbury thorn tree, grown from a cutting from the original tree at Glastonbury in England, which is said to have been planted by Joseph of Arimathea. The bishop's garden, a lovely place, is entered through a twelfth century Norman arch that was brought from France, and the great boxwood tree, more than two centuries old, the yew trees, the holly, and the blossoming flowers make a living picture of a medieval garden.

At the southwest corner of the cathedral grounds, Massachusetts Avenue crosses busy Wisconsin Avenue, and then goes on past the 80 acre campus of the College of Liberal Arts of the American University. Hillcrest, the "Children's Village" of the Washington Orphan Asylum, comes next, and then this great avenue reaches Massachusetts Portal, the District-Maryland boundary line. Not stopping there, Massachusetts Avenue continues through attractive suburbs for three miles, almost to Glen Echo —which is a popular amusement park, named for the nearby home of Clara Barton, the founder of the American Red Cross Association.

CHAPTER

# Sixteenth Street

The most important residential street in the capital is Sixteenth, with its 6½ miles extending in a straight line north from Lafayette Square to the District of Columbia-Maryland boundary at Blair Portal.

As one travels on this long thoroughfare, the unusual method of naming the streets extending east and west is easily discovered. After all letters of the alphabet have been used, the cross streets are given one-syllable names, the first letters of which agree with the order of the alphabet. The second series of streets has two-syllable names, with the first letters in alphabetical order, the third series has three-syllable names, in the same arrangement, and the fourth group has names of flowers and trees.

For almost its entire length Sixteenth Street is lined with churches, hotels, huge apartment buildings, the national headquarters of various organizations, and the imposing residences of ambassadors and ministers from foreign countries.

### St. John's Episcopal Church

This is one of the oldest as well as one of the most famous churches in Washington. It is opposite Lafayette Square, the first building on the right side of Sixteenth Street. Its bell was made in the famous Paul Revere foundry.

It has been customary to reserve a pew here for the President of the United States, and for that reason, and perhaps also because of its proximity to the White House, St. John's is often spoken of as the President's church. Number 54 was President Franklin D. Roosevelt's pew.

### National Geographic Society

This society has its headquarters at Sixteenth and M Streets. Like the Smithsonian Institution, the organization is dedicated to "the increase and diffusion of knowledge." Organized in 1888, it is now recognized as having the largest membership of any society in the world. It is an international group, having subscribers in every country of the world.

The Geographic Society has sponsored scores of expeditions and has sent hundreds of scientists, explorers, and specialists all over the globe. The stories of their travels and the reports of their discoveries have been described and illustrated in the "National Geographic Magazine" which is sent to all members of the organization every month.

### Foundry Methodist Church

This church at Sixteenth and P Streets received its unusual name from an event in Washington history. During the War of 1812, Henry Foxhall made most of the arms and ammunition for the American forces in his foundry above Georgetown, near Little Falls. He was desperately afraid that the British might discover the foundry and destroy it, with all the weapons which the Americans had stored there.

As the English soldiers approached the capital city, on August 24, 1814, Foxhall's fears increased. Being a devout man, he prayed for help, promising that if his foundry were spared from destruction he would build a fine church to show his gratitude to God. The British were stopped in their attack on Washington by a violent tornado and cloudburst. The foundry was unmolested, and Foxhall felt that his prayers had been answered. True to his vow, he immediately had a large church built at the corner of Fourteenth and G Streets, and called it the Foundry Church. Gradually shops and stores surrounded it, and later a new church was built on the present site, well out of the business district.

### Scottish Rite Masonic Temple

The Scottish Rite 33rd Degree Masonic Temple is built after the style of the tomb of King Mausolus. The word "mausoleum" is derived from the name of this king whose tomb was considered one of the seven wonders of the ancient world.

Every part of this building has a special significance for the Masons; the 33 Ionic columns, each 33 feet high, are symbolic of the 33 degrees of Masonry. There are 33 rooms on the main floor, and innumerable objects of symbolism in the various rooms in the building. There is an extensive library in this temple containing, among other literary treasures, an unusual collection of most of the works of Robert Burns.

The two sphinxes guarding the entrance symbolize power and divine wisdom. Even the steps from the street to the main entrance are in groupings of 1-3-5-7-9, the sacred numbers of ancient times.

### Meridian Hill Park

The most beautiful formal park in the city, this is named for its location—on the first meridian. The point is marked at the end of the park near Sixteenth Street and Florida Avenue.

A meridian, as geographies teach, is an imaginary line extending through the north and south poles and passing through a given point on the earth's surface. From a prime meridian the longitude, or the distance east and west between two places, is measured. Greenwich, England, and Washington, D.C., are the prime meridians.

In 1804, President Thomas Jefferson had the first meridian line run from the north down Sixteenth Street, through the north door of the White House, and on south through the grounds. The Zero Milestone in the Ellipse is on the meridian line.

In the early days it was customary for nations to establish a meridian line through their own capitals, and from there to reckon the distances to various points.

Meridian Hill Park covers 12 acres and is enclosed by a concrete wall, terraced on two levels. The upper part ends in a grand terrace from which there is a splendid view to the south over the city. At the north end there is a spectacular waterfall, from three fountains set in large niches in the wall, cascading down a dozen or more steps to a small pool, then on to a large reflecting pool in the lower level of the garden.

There are several interesting statues decorating the park; the most outstanding is that of Joan of Arc, given to the women of America by the French women of New York City. It is an exact copy of the statue by Paul Dubois before Rheims Cathedral, which is recognized as one of the finest modern equestrian statues.

### All Souls' Unitarian Church

On the right, at the corner of Harvard and Sixteenth Streets, this church is reminiscent of St. Martin's-in-the-Fields in London, with its red brick trimmed with white stone, the lofty clock tower, and, high at the tip of the spire, the gilded weather vane. The bell in this tower was cast in the famous Paul Revere foundry.

### Washington Chapel

The Church of the Latter Day Saints is at Sixteenth Street and Columbia Road. This structure is the only building in the world made of the white bird's-eye marble of Utah. Atop the spire, which is a replica of the one on the Mormon Temple in Salt Lake City, is the graceful figure of the angel Moroni.

### Army Medical Center; Walter Reed Army Hospital

The Army Medical Center and the Walter Reed Army Hospital are near the end of the $6\frac{1}{2}$ miles of Sixteenth Street. The hospital was named in honor of Dr. Walter Reed who heroically proved that mosquitoes carry the virus of yellow fever. In the vast Army Medical Center, medical and surgical treatment is available to sick and wounded soldiers. The surroundings are beautiful, with trees, shrubs, flowers, fountains, and unusual gardens adding their charm to this place of healing.

### United States Chamber of Commerce

This building at the northeast corner of H Street and Connecticut Avenue, opposite Lafayette Square, is on the site of the former residence of Daniel Webster.

One day in the year 1768, 20 New York merchants met in Bolton and Spiegel's Tavern, to talk over business conditions and to make plans which would benefit trade in the Colonies. Then and there the first business association in America was formed. It was called the New York Chamber of Commerce and it received a charter from King George III of England two years later. Then, in 1784, the United States Congress granted a charter to the organization.

President Taft and the Secretary of the Department of Commerce and Labor invited the business leaders of the country to meet with them in Washington in 1912. At that meeting was formed the greatest organization of commercial interests in the world—the United States Chamber of Commerce. Its principal purpose is "to serve business by encouraging trade and commerce—not only between the states and territories of the United States, but also with foreign countries." Today every city and town of any size in America has its own chamber of commerce.

In 1925 the Chamber of Commerce of the United States built its headquarters in Washington, D.C. Cass Gilbert, who later designed the Supreme Court Building, planned the $3,000,000 structure, and 13,500 businessmen and firms, in every part of the country, paid for it.

Carved on the frieze of this building, above the courtyard, is this appropriate quotation from one of Daniel Webster's speeches: "Let us develop the resources of our land, call forth its powers, build up its institutions, promote all its great interests, and see whether we also, in our day and generation, may not perform something worthy to be remembered."

## National Bureau of Standards

The National Bureau of Standards buildings, 99 in number, are located on a wooded tract of 68 acres on Connecticut Avenue and Van Ness Street. The 71 sections, scientific and technical, work to advance the various branches of the sciences. The Bureau also protects the Government and the citizens of the United States from being cheated by false weights, measures, and values. It is under the Department of Commerce. Although of fairly recent origin, it is now the largest, most comprehensive bureau of standards in the world.

The need for a system of measurement was recognized when our Government was first planned. Both the Articles of Confederation and the Constitution allotted to Congress "the power of fixing the standards of weights and measures throughout the Country." But Congress did not act quickly in the matter. Four presidents, George Washington, Thomas Jefferson, James Madison, and John Quincy Adams, in turn, vainly tried to stir Congress to adopt unified standards of measurement. In the meantime, people went on with the "nose-to-thumb" measure. This was an old-time custom of measuring a yard by the distance from the tip of the nose, along the outstretched arm, to the end of the thumb. It was called a yard, whether the arm was long or short.

Finally, in 1889, our Government purchased from the International Bureau of Weights and Measures in Paris a standard of weight called a kilogram and a standard of length called a meter. These priceless treasures, kept in a well guarded vault at the Bureau of Standards, enable the Bureau to maintain a fundamental system of weights and measures all over the country, so that now a yard is 36 inches from Texas to Maine.

The Bureau of Standards employs hundreds of workers who are engaged in research in science and industry, and they have perfected countless valuable inventions. One of the latest is the "radiosonde," now one of the chief aids of the United States Weather Bureau. Radiosondes are miniature, automatic radio-transmitting devices. They are attached to small balloons and sent up 50,000 to 75,000 feet in the air, where they record the temperature, humidity, and velocity and direction of the wind. These recordings are picked up on the ground by automatic receiving sets, and are particularly useful to airline services.

The National Bureau of Standards has the greatest testing laboratories in the world. They have machines so powerful that they can break heavy steel girders apart, and others so sensitive and delicate that they can weigh 1/50,000,000th of a pound, or measure 1/1,000,000th of an inch. There are three buildings called "wind tunnels," where powerful blasts of air rush through at 75 to 180 miles an hour, to test such things as bombs, bridges, or towers.

Samples are tested and standards are established for everything purchased by the Government. The services of the Bureau are available without charge to all departments of the Government, but outsiders—individuals or organizations—must pay a fee to the Treasury Department for all tests. In the great laboratories are machines to test such diverse articles as stockings, shoes, pins, paint, food, fabrics, and motors. Everything must meet the Government standards of measurement, quality, and performance.

## Zoological Park

The zoo, on Connecticut Avenue, with its main entrance near Hawthorne Street, is one of Washington's most popular attractions. It is really a department of the Smithsonian Institution, and it began with the surplus number of animals that were kept for use as models for the taxidermists. The "models' " large families soon became a nuisance in their makeshift quarters on the Mall. Mr. William Hornaday, the Smithsonian taxidermist, saw the possibility of using the animals as a nucleus for a zoological collection and urged the purchase of suitable land for the purpose. The park was established "for the advancement of science and the instruction and recreation of the people."

The tract of land on Rock Creek was bought, and in 1890 the National Zoological Garden was begun, on a small scale. Now 176 acres are used to house the thousands of animals belonging to the zoo. Great care has been taken to make the housing conditions, including the temperatures, perfectly suited to the various inhabitants. The reptile house is said to be the model for zoos all over the world, and numerous scientists and zoologists from many foreign countries have come to inspect it.

One of the most popular residents of the zoo is "Smoky," a brown bear who was rescued from a disastrous forest fire in the mountains in the West. The cunning little cub was brought to Washington by a friendly airplane pilot. The baby bear's coat was singed and his feet were scorched. He was given the best of care and made friends quickly. Smoky looked like a live Teddy bear and delighted his admiring audience with his antics.

There are birds of all sizes, kinds, and colors; perhaps the most unattractive is the adjutant bird from India. He is a stork, 4 feet high, with a bald head, and he stands in an uncomfortable, hunched-up position, spending most of his time in apparently deep meditation.

The largest bird flight-cage harbors a group of black-crowned night herons. A colony of 100 wild specimens of this native bird has made its permanent home in the park, supposedly to keep its captive relatives company. The antarctic penguins are kept in an air-conditioned cage. The industrious beaver colony is constantly at work on a dam in their pond. They have been on this job for more than 20 years.

It would take reams of paper to describe all of the interesting inhabitants of the zoo; and to see them all would take months, but there would never be a dull moment.

## Rock Creek Park

Rock Creek Park extends 4 miles beyond the zoo, and contains more than 1,800 acres. On these acres are forests, open fields, high cliffs, winding driveways, and bridle paths; while through the length of the park, Rock Creek, twisting and turning, makes its way to join the waters of the Potomac.

Rock Creek Park is a marvelous playground, with places for all types of recreation: three golf courses, tennis courts, baseball diamonds, and picnic grounds.

The cabin of Joaquin Miller, the poet of the Sierras, is now in Rock Creek Park; it was formerly in Meridian Hill Park on Sixteenth Street. The Pierce Mill is another landmark in the park. It was built in 1829, and excellent water-ground corn meal is still produced by this old mill.

Lord Bryce, a former British ambassador to the United States, was most enthusiastic over the beauty of the park. In an article on Washington, he wrote: "To Rock Creek there is nothing comparable in any capital city of Europe."

CHAPTER

# 12

## Georgetown and Outlying Points

Georgetown begins where Pennsylvania Avenue crosses Rock Creek and merges into M Street. There is no dividing line, as Georgetown is really a part of Washington—officially West Washington—but Georgetown residents do not care to give up the original name.

Georgetown is old and is proud of its antiquity. It was built on the site of Tohoga, an Indian village. When people began to buy land and build houses in this vicinity, they called it the "Town of George." The question often asked is: for which George was the town named? There was, first of all, King George; then the great landowners, George Beall and George Gordon; while many claimed that it was named in honor of George Washington. It could not possibly have been named for Washington, as he was only a lad in his teens, with no claim to fame, in 1751 when the town was surveyed and laid out. Nor were Beall and Gordon in line for such honor. Therefore it is generally conceded that the town was named for King George II, who was then the ruler of England and her colonies in North America.

Georgetown soon became a thriving tobacco-shipping port where large ships anchored in the bay at Rock Creek, to load their cargoes for foreign lands. Tobacco was the money of the colonists. In 1789, Georgetown was incorporated, and wealthy planters were building fine homes up on the "Heights" where they had a wide view of the Potomac River and the Virginia hills beyond. "Rolling houses" were found on many of these estates. A "rolling house" was a large, weatherproof barn in which tobacco was stored before it was sold or shipped. They were so called from the "rolling" roads over which large casks of tobacco were taken to the market. An axle ran through the center of the cask. Shafts were attached to the ends of the axle, and Negro slaves or horses between the shafts pulled the casks.

M Street is disappointing, with its motley array of little stores and shops, but all Georgetown must not be judged from these first blocks on M Street. There are hundreds of beautiful houses in this town of long ago. Old Georgetown proper is the section off M Street, up to the Heights. N, O, P, Q, and R Streets all are bordered by fine old residences, some small and ivy-covered, and some large and handsome, standing aloof in their beautiful grounds. Georgetown hasn't cared to become modernized but has preferred to restore the old houses and preserve them in the style of their original period.

At 1239 Thirtieth Street is Georgetown's smallest house, only 11 feet wide. It was built, it is said, for spite, to shut out the daylight from the house next door.

### Dumbarton House

The house at 2715 Q Street was built soon after the Revolutionary War. It is the home of the National Society of Colonial Dames. Beautifully and richly furnished, in accordance with the period of 1780 to 1800, it also has a small museum with many interesting exhibits. It is open to visitors upon the payment of a small fee.

### Dumbarton Oaks

Dumbarton Oaks, at 3101 R. Street, is one of the largest estates in the District of Columbia. The great mansion stands in a magnificent setting of grand old trees, and elaborately landscaped gardens with a yew walk, a picturesque stream, and waterfalls. Both the interior and exterior were often photographed when the international conference for establishing a general international organization met there in September 1944 and laid the foundations of the United Nations. A few years previously the owners, Mr. and Mrs. Robert Woods Bliss, had presented this property to Harvard University, to use for graduate study in diplomacy.

### Tudor House

At Q and Thirty-first Streets is Tudor House, often called Georgetown's most elegant residence. It was built by Thomas Peter for his wife, Martha Parke Custis, Martha Washington's granddaughter. Dr. Thornton, the designer of the Capitol, planned it. The house is beautiful and the wonderful old trees and acres of velvety lawns add to its grandeur.

### Hurst Home for the Blind

Mr. and Mrs. Henry Hurst left their home at 3050 R Street and an endowment fund to establish a home for the blind. Braille and basket-weaving and other handicrafts are taught here. Any blind person in the District is eligible but only approximately 40 can be accommodated.

### Dumbarton Bridge

This bridge over Rock Creek, where it is crossed by Massachusetts Avenue, is worth seeing. It is one of the few curving bridges in the United States, and the bronze buffaloes at either side of the entrance are fine sculptures by Saint-Gaudens.

### Georgetown University

At Thirty-seventh and N Streets, high on the bluffs above the Potomac River, with a most extensive view, is the oldest Roman Catholic college in the United States. It was founded in 1789 by Father John Carroll, the first Catholic Bishop of Baltimore, and a cousin of Charles Carroll, one of the signers of the Declaration of Independence. Bishop Carroll's statue in bronze stands in front of the main building.

### Convent of the Visitation

This academy for girls was founded in 1799 by Leonard Neale, the second Archbishop of Baltimore. It is on the east side of grounds of Georgetown University.

### Volta Bureau

The Volta Bureau at 1537 Thirty-fifth Street, across the road from the Convent of the Visitation, is an institution whose name is known throughout the United States. It was established for the education of the deaf.

Alexander Graham Bell, a teacher of the deaf, married one of his pupils. While working on an instrument to improve her hearing, Bell perfected his idea for the telephone. For this useful invention he received the much coveted Volta Prize which was established in 1801 when Napoleon I awarded a prize of $10,000 to the great Italian scientist, Count Volte, the inventor of the electric battery. This prize was given his name.

With the money he received from his graphophone invention and the Volta Prize money, Alexander Graham Bell founded and endowed the Volta Bureau. Helen Keller broke the soil for the building in 1893, on a lot across the street from Bell's home.

The Volta Bureau has become the headquarters of the American Association to Promote the Teaching of Speech to the Deaf. It also is the headquarters of the American Federation of Organizations for the Hard of Hearing.

### Griffith Stadium

The sports center of Washington is located at Florida Avenue and Seventh Street, Northwest. It is well known to all baseball fans as the home of the famous team, the Senators.

### Howard University

This university for Negroes was established in 1867. Its campus is just north of the Griffith Stadium, at 2401 Sixth Street, Northwest. Howard University is the foremost institution of higher education for the colored people of the United States, and is maintained by appropriations from Congress and through private contributions. Its divisions include a law school, a school of religion, and a college of medicine.

### Soldiers' Home

Four miles directly north of the Capitol, on First Street, in a beautiful setting of 500 acres, is the oldest soldiers' home in the United States.

A home for old soldiers had been proposed to Congress as early as 1829, and again in 1840. But nothing was accomplished until General Winfield Scott, nicknamed "Old Fuss and Feathers," gave $100,000, which he had collected as tribute from the City of Mexico when it failed to keep the truce with the United States in the Mexican War. The site of the Soldiers' Home was purchased with General Scott's gift.

The location of the Home is particularly fine, with a view of old Sugar Loaf Mountain 60 miles distant in the hills of Maryland. It is much cooler here than in downtown Washington, and several of the Presidents have used the Soldiers' Home as their summer quarters; Buchanan, Lincoln, Hayes, and Arthur were among the number.

### St. Paul's Church and Rock Creek Cemetery

On Rock Creek Church Road, adjoining the Soldiers' Home, are the oldest church and the oldest cemetery in the District of Columbia, both founded in 1712.

Many well known men and women are buried in this quiet spot. Here the famous monument to the memory of Mrs. Henry Adams is located. This bronze statue is the work of the great sculptor, Augustus Saint-Gaudens, and is considered one of America's finest works of art.

### Catholic University of America

Founded by Pope Leo XIII, in 1887, this is the greatest center of culture and learning for Roman Catholics in

America. Between Taylor Street and Michigan Avenue, it is located just east of the grounds of the Soldiers' Home, on a tract of 70 acres, formerly an estate called Middleton Manor.

Like the universities of the Middle Ages, Catholic University is a concentration of religious communities and houses of study, such as colleges, schools, convents, seminaries, friaries, and monasteries. There are sixty five buildings on the grounds.

Catholic University is noted for its Drama and Theater Department where many plays are successfully written and produced, and for its library of 450,000 volumes.

### Columbia Institute for the Deaf

On Seventh Street, Northwest, and Florida Avenue is one of Washington's most important and unusual educational institutions. As the Columbia Institute for the Deaf, Dumb and Blind, it was incorporated in 1857, given a large appropriation by Congress, and managed by the Government. Later the title was changed to the Columbia Institute for the Deaf. The college was named for the famous teacher of the deaf, Dr. Thomas H. Gallaudet, and was granted the authority to give degrees by President Lincoln in 1864.

The Institute owns 103 acres of land, including a fine campus of 20 acres and a 40 acre farm that produces supplies for the school. Eighteen large buildings are grouped in the spacious grounds.

Three different schools make up this institution of learning: the Kendall School which gives courses of instruction from kindergarten through high school; Gallaudet College, offering a four year course with B.A. and B.S. degrees; and the Normal Training Department which instructs college graduates (including those from other schools and

with unimpaired hearing) in the teaching of the deaf.
Gallaudet College is the only school in the world which
offers higher education to the deaf, and it attracts students
from almost every foreign land.

## Washington Navy Yard

The Navy Yard is at Eighth and M Streets, Southeast,
on the Anacostia River. This is one of the six Navy yards
planned in John Adams' administration.

In 1800, the Government bought 37 acres of land for
$4,000; the yard now covers 115 acres. The Washington
Navy Yard became noted for excellence in ordnance design. The famous *Hornet* and *Wasp* were constructed here.
There is an interesting yard museum where a number of
rare guns and cannon may be seen.

## Anacostia Park

Anacostia Park extends over 1,000 acres on both sides
of the Anacostia River, from the Navy Yard to the District-Maryland boundary, approximately 5 miles away.
Archaeologists have made many interesting finds in the
Anacostia region, some of them dating before Columbus'
discovery of America. They have found 32 varieties of soil
in this area.

# ⚑ 13 ⚑

# The Potomac River: Bridges, Falls, and Canals

## *Arlington Memorial Bridge*

This bridge is west of the Lincoln Memorial at the foot of the Mall. A bridge at this point had long been needed. A full century before it was built, President Andrew Jackson asked that "a memorial bridge be built across the Potomac River as a symbol of the firmly established Union of the North and South." But on November 11, 1921, the day of the burial of the "Unknown Soldier," the need for a bridge was apparent to all of the many thousands who attended the ceremony. Such a traffic jam had never been known before. The public protested loudly and long. Congress rushed into action and made appropriations. Plans were prepared. Work was started in 1926 and the Arlington Memorial Bridge was opened January 18, 1932.

The bridge is a magnificent one. Although it was built as low as possible to avoid interfering with the view from the Lincoln Memorial or the Lee House at Arlington, it is in perfect proportion. The bridge is 2,138 feet long and its width of 90 feet is divided into six lanes. This is said to be the world's largest drawbridge. The spans are of North Carolina granite, as Jackson had wished them to be. The pylons, 35 feet in height, are topped by great eagles, 18 feet high, each cut from one solid block of the stone. The bridge leads directly from the Lincoln Memorial Plaza to the Lee House, the Memorial Amphitheater, and the Tomb of the Unknown Soldier.

In 1929 the Commission of Fine Arts recommended that equestrian statues be erected at the entrance to the Arlington Memorial Bridge and at the approaches to the Rock Creek and Potomac Parkway. A national competition to select the sculptors and the subjects was won by two well known American sculptors, Leo Friedlander and James Earle Fraser.

They were commissioned to begin the work on August 1, 1931, but several unforeseen occurrences delayed their completion. The depression years caused the first interference. Then when the small granite models were finished in 1938, the sculptors and the architects decided that the statues must be made of bronze instead of stone. Restrictions on metal during World War II banned the use of bronze and other metals, and it was not until ten years later (1948) that the full-sized plaster models were completed.

At that time the Italian Ambassador informed the United States Government that his country asked to be allowed to cast and gild the four statues as "a gesture of good will" toward the American people from the people of Italy. This offer was gladly accepted. The 150 pieces composing the plaster models of the four great statues were carefully crated, stored in two ships, and sent from New York to Italy on February 1, 1950.

The four statues were cast and finished in four different Italian foundries, in Naples, Rome, Milan, and Florence. The casting and gilding required 14 months. Most of this time was occupied in applying the "fire-gilt" finish, an ancient method of fusing gold onto the bronze by use of intense heat. One hundred pounds of 24-carat gold were used in covering the four statues. They were the largest statues that were ever "fire-gilt."

This work was completed in 1951. The four statues, in one ship, sailed from Leghorn, Italy, May 20th, arriving in Norfolk, Virginia, June 1st. From there, they were shipped by barge up the Potomac River to Washington, D.C., and placed permanently by June 19th.

On September 26, 1951, a formal ceremony of dedication was held at the Arlington Memorial Bridge Plaza. The United States Army Band and the Naval Academy Band gave a concert. Ezio Pinza, the famous Metropolitan Opera star, sang. His Excellency, Alcide de Gasperi, the Premier of Italy, presented the gift to Harry S. Truman, the President of the United States. The sculptors unveiled their statues: Friedlander, the creator of the groups at the entrance to the bridge, "Valor" and "Sacrifice," symbolizing the Arts of War, and Fraser, his figures "Music and Harvest," "Aspiration and Literature," symbolizing the Arts of Peace.

### Theodore Roosevelt Island

Theodore Roosevelt Island lies in the Potomac River not far from the Arlington Memorial Bridge. This pear-shaped island of approximately 75 acres is a deserted spot now, but in years long past it was the site of a fine home, filled with guests and gaiety.

In 1932 the island was given to the Government to be established as a Theodore Roosevelt Memorial. Someday the tangled wilderness may become a beautiful island park in memory of this President who loved the great outdoors.

## Key Bridge

The Francis Scott Key Bridge crosses the Potomac River at Thirty-fifth Street in Georgetown and ends in Rosslyn, Virginia. A few doors to the left of the bridge entrance stood the Key residence, a large brick house, where the Keys and their six sons and five daughters lived. It was an attractive place, with trees, shrubs, a well tended lawn, and a lovely garden sloping down to the bank of the river, but the house was torn down years ago and there is now only a lot overgrown with weeds.

Behind the old Key house the remains of the original Aqueduct Bridge can be seen. This bridge was built to enable canal boats to cross the Potomac. A wooden trough, wide enough for a regular canal boat, was laid on top of eight massive masonry piers. This trough, filled with water, made it possible to run the canal boats from one side of the river to the other. Another bridge, also of wood, was built over the top of the canal bridge, for the use of vehicles. This two-storied structure was opened in 1843, but it was never a success as it needed constant repairs. An iron bridge replaced it in 1888. The Francis Scott Key Bridge was built in 1923.

While Key was living in this house, our national anthem was written. After the British raid on Washington on August 23, 1814, Admiral Cockburn and his troops had marched back to the fleet in Chesapeake Bay. Key, who had been a volunteer aide in the defense of the capital, had returned to his home in Georgetown. It was here, a week later, that Richard West arrived to ask Key to go to the rescue of Dr. William Beanes, Key's friend living in

Upper Marlboro, Maryland. Beanes was a prisoner on the British fleet.

Key sent his wife and children, in the care of their faithful coachman, to Terra Rubra, his home near Frederick, Maryland. He then visited President Madison to obtain official permission to ask for Beanes' release. Armed with this request from the President and a letter from General Winder, head of the American forces, Francis Key set out in his carriage for the full day's trip to Baltimore.

All of Key's talents as a lawyer were needed in his arguments with Admiral Cockburn, but he finally secured the admiral's promise that Dr. Beanes would be set free. However, there was one restriction: both Beanes and Key must remain on the ship during the British bombardment of Fort McHenry, near Baltimore. It was that long night of watching and praying for the safety of the American fort that inspired Francis Scott Key, who was a poet as well as a lawyer, to write "The Star-Spangled Banner." He scribbled most of the words on an old letter which he had in his pocket, and completed the poem after he reached land.

### Chain Bridge

The Chain Bridge is near Little Falls, about 3 miles above the Francis Scott Key Bridge. It was on this very spot that the first bridge across the Potomac in this section was built, in 1797. This was a covered, wooden bridge which deteriorated from constant use after seven years. Immediately, a second one was built, a duplicate of the first, but in six months it was washed out by spring floods.

Four years later, in 1809, a new bridge at this same location was hung by iron chains. For this reason it was called the Chain Bridge. It was thought that this would be a lasting structure, but the huge logs, swept from upstream, tore it down in two years.

A new bridge, also suspended by chains, built in 1811, was a toll bridge until 1833. No matter how it is constructed, any and every bridge that may be built here will always be called the "Chain Bridge."

## Cabin John Bridge

When this granite and sandstone arch was built over Cabin John's Creek (1855 to 1860) it was said to be one of the longest masonry arches in the world. It was a part of the aqueduct system of the District of Columbia water works, and it still carries the original water conduit.

The building of Cabin John Bridge was begun under the supervision of Jefferson Davis, then Secretary of War in President Pierce's cabinet, the same Jeff Davis who a few years later became the President of the Confederate States of America. His name and that of Captain Meigs, the Army engineer in charge of the work, were inscribed on the bridge. During the Civil War, feeling against the South ran so high that someone scratched off Jefferson Davis' name, but 46 years later President Theodore Roosevelt had it restored.

The unusual name, "Cabin John," came from "Captain John" who lived in a log cabin near the stream called "Cabin John's Creek." He was a peculiar man who was known as a hermit. He was believed to have been a pirate and to have buried his treasures in the area. So firmly was this idea established in people's minds that, in the early years, anyone buying land in the vicinity had to sign a written agreement to share equally with the original owner any treasure found or dug up on the land. The name "Captain John" was gradually garbled into "Cabin John."

This section abounds in many varieties of wild flowers, and every spring visitors to Washington are attracted by the unusual signs displayed on the street cars: "Beautiful

Spring! Birds are singing! Flowers are blooming along the Potomac! Take Cabin John Car."

### Great Falls

The Great Falls of the Potomac is one of the most beautiful natural scenic spots in the Washington area; it is about 13 miles from the city. This is not a direct, abrupt waterfall, but a long series of roaring cataracts and foaming rapids, plunging and leaping over huge piles of enormous granite rocks and cliffs. The shores near the falls are thickly wooded, but there is a large cleared section, Great Falls Park, on the Virginia side of the river.

Here in the park can be seen the ruins of the old mill and the iron foundry once owned by George Washington. There are also traces of the Potomac Canal, now a shallow, weedy ditch; a portion of it still contains water. Tables, benches, and fireplaces entice nature-loving picnickers, and refreshment and amusement stands offer their attractions. On the Maryland side of the river, near the towpath, is the old Great Falls Tavern, built about 1829. A short walk takes one to the top of the high, rocky bank for a fine view of the falls and the river below.

Great Falls Park will be more accessible when the plans of the Park Commission are carried out. The George Washington Memorial Parkway, a continuous, landscaped drive, will extend along the shores of the Potomac River from Fort Washington to Great Falls on the Maryland side and from Mount Vernon to Great Falls on the Virginia side of the river.

### Chesapeake and Ohio Canal

The old canal begins at the turn of the Potomac River in Georgetown.

When George Washington was a young man of 22, he began to plan a canal, to utilize the Potomac River as an important waterway connecting the East with the Western Territory. He planned for a canal from Georgetown to Cumberland, Maryland, then on to Pittsburgh and the Ohio Valley. There were neither highways nor railways in those days; the only available means of travel and transportation was by water.

Washington continued to think, plan, and talk about his idea of a canal, and in 1785, the "Potowmack" Canal Company was organized and chartered. George Washington owned a great deal of the stock, and—not because of that, but because he had made the plans—he was elected as the first president of the company. Although he resigned from this office when he became the President of the United States, he continued to be actively interested in the Canal as long as he lived.

The "Potowmack" Canal began to operate in 1802, using the canal channel when the river was not deep or wide enough for the boats. The venture prospered, and many loads of flour, furs, and lumber were hauled back and forth on the new waterway in rafts and boats of all sorts. Then, in 1826, the Chesapeake and Ohio Canal Company bought the old Potowmack Company and prepared to extend the canal to Pittsburgh, as Washington had planned.

On July 4, 1828, President John Quincy Adams turned the first spadeful of earth, to extend the canal to Pittsburgh, a distance of 360 miles. The Chesapeake and Ohio Canal never reached Pittsburgh, but it did go as far as Cumberland, Maryland, 184 miles from Washington, and a lively traffic flowed between its banks. Hundreds of boats plied up and down the canal for almost a full century, until the railroads and other more rapid means of transportation came into general use. The Chesapeake and Ohio

Canal Company suspended business in 1924, and 14 years later the Government purchased the property.

The National Park Service has restored the old canal for 22 miles—from Georgetown to Seneca, Maryland—and today you can enjoy a trip by canal boat, drawn by mules along the tow path, in the leisurely manner of olden times.

## 🏴 14 🏴

# Down the Mount Vernon Memorial Highway

### The Lee Mansion

On the heights above the Potomac River, across from the Lincoln Memorial, is the stately Lee Mansion, or Arlington House as it was formerly called. This estate originally belonged to John Parke Custis, Martha Washington's son by her first husband. It was named Arlington, after the Custis' ancestral home in Northampton County, Virginia.

Young John Parke Custis, while serving as aide-de-camp to his stepfather, General Washington, in the Revolutionary War, died of camp fever in 1781. Arlington was left to his little son, George Washington Parke Custis. George Washington and his wife adopted the little boy and his sister Nellie, and reared them at Mount Vernon, caring for them and loving them as if they were their own children.

On top of the long, sloping hill at Arlington, George

Washington built a small summer home which he occupied while supervising the early work on the Federal City, for Mount Vernon was 16 miles away, a long horseback ride to take twice a day. Later the house burned, and it was on this beautiful site that George Washington Parke Custis built Arlington House in 1802. It has often been cited as one of the finest specimens of federal architecture in the United States, and it is perfectly suited to its magnificent location.

Custis married charming Mary Fitzhugh, and for almost 50 years Arlington House was the gay center of social life in Washington and the vicinity. General Lafayette was entertained there a number of times during his visits to America. But the most joyous occasion was on June 30, 1831, when Mary Ann Randolph Custis, the only surviving child of the Custises, was married to Lieutenant Robert E. Lee, of Stratford, Virginia. The wedding was an elaborate affair; the bridal pair stood under a huge floral bell hung in the center arch between the family dining room and the parlor. The gay young people in the wedding party stayed on and made merry for a whole week. Lieutenant Lee and his bride made their home at Arlington.

Thirty years later General Robert E. Lee left this house forever, to take command of the Confederate Army. Arlington became an armed camp during the Civil War and later, in 1883, the United States Government bought the entire estate for $150,000 and set aside 200 acres for the National Cemetery. Fort Myer had been previously established in permanent quarters on an adjoining part of the Lee estate.

For many years only a part of the mansion was used as an office and residence by the superintendent of the cemetery. The remaining rooms were bare and the whole house was giving way to ruin and decay. Finally, Congress approved a request which had been expressed by people from all parts of the United States: that the mansion be restored and preserved as a national memorial to gallant General Robert E. Lee.

The Quartermaster Corps of the United States Army began the work of restoration, rebuilding and refurnishing the house as it was originally—as a home, not a museum. Some of the furniture known to have been in the house originally was obtained, some pieces were copied, and a few articles were returned voluntarily by families who had gained possession of them.

This lovely, spacious house, furnished throughout as it was during the Lees' residence, gives a faithful picture of the gracious manner of life in a refined American home of the mid-nineteenth century. That the people of the United States like to see this famous memorial is evidenced by the half million visitors who go there every year.

### Arlington National Cemetery

With the opening of the Civil War, the Arlington estate, the famous home of Robert E. Lee, was used as an Army camp. Age-old trees and the beautiful grounds were sacrificed to make room for barracks, hospitals, and army tents. When the necessity arose for a permanent national cemetery in 1864, 200 acres near the mansion were reserved for this purpose. Later this was increased to 408 acres.

Ten gates provide entrances to the Arlington Cemetery; the main entrance is the Court of Honor and Memorial Gate, honoring the members of the Army, Navy, Coast Guard, and Marine branches of the Armed services. Their respective emblems are on the tall iron gates. This entrance begins at the great plaza near the Virginia end of the Arlington Memorial Bridge and is marked on each side by pylons topped with eagles, matching those at the end of the Memorial Bridge.

The tomb of Major L'Enfant is in a prominent spot, immediately in front of the Lee Mansion, on the brow of the hill overlooking the beautiful city which he had planned. William Howard Taft, the only President buried in Arlington, rests a little farther down the slope; and the grave of Robert Todd Lincoln, the son of President Lincoln, is nearby.

On May 30, 1868, General John A Logan, Commander in Chief of the Grand Army of the Republic, held the first official Memorial Day services on the front portico of the Lee Mansion. Each year more and more people attended these services, and in 1888 Memorial Day was declared a legal holiday.

The portico was soon too small to hold the crowd, and for several years the people gathered in an open space in a grove of maple trees on the grounds, which was called Sylvan Hall. After that, the services were held in the large wistaria-covered arbor, not far from the house. During World War I, the erection of an amphitheater and chapel was begun; it was completed and dedicated May 15, 1920.

The white marble amphitheater was built as a memorial to the heroic members of the Army, Navy, and Marine forces whose lives had been lost in World War I. This theater is elliptical, enclosed by tall, marble columns and an arcade. It has a seating capacity of 4,000. There are a roomy stage and entrance hall, a museum on the second floor, and a chapel in the basement. Underneath the colonnade are 48 crypts, intended for the resting places of 48 men—one from each state in the Union—who have given outstanding service to their country.

### The Tomb of the Unknown Soldier

East of the main entrance of the amphitheater, on a broad, marble terrace, is the Tomb of the Unknown Soldier. It is ideally located. A wide, grassy slope, with walks at either side, leads up to the flight of granite steps which end at the paved terrace across the front of the Memorial Amphitheater. In the center of the space at the head of the steps is a sarcophagus of snowy, Colorado yule marble, the tomb of the unknown American soldier whose body was brought home from a cemetery in France. This is how that particular soldier was selected:

After World War I, four United States Army officers each chose a coffin containing the body of a private soldier from among the many thousands of unidentified American soldiers buried near the French battlefields. One casket was taken from Bony, one from Romagne, one from Thraucourt, and one from Belleau Wood. They were all carried to the City Hall in Châlons-sur-Marne. A sergeant, Edward F. Younger of Chicago, was asked to select the coffin to be sent to America.

The solemn strains of Chopin's Funeral March were played by a band outside the hall as Sergeant Younger entered the room, carrying an armful of white roses. He looked hesitantly at the four caskets—one by one—and finally, he laid the roses on one coffin and hurriedly left the room. An American officer stepped forward and placed a copper plate below the flowers. It was inscribed:

"An Unknown American
Who gave his life in the World War."

The flag-draped coffin was placed on the deck of the battleship *Olympia,* Admiral Dewey's flagship, with four American sailors who had won honors in the war as the guard of honor.

The *Olympia* docked at the Navy Yard in Washington, November 10, 1921, and an impressive Army escort bore the casket to the Capitol to lie in state in the great rotunda. There, thousands came to pay silent tribute to the unknown hero. The next day, Armistice Day, November 11, 1921, a stately procession, the highest officials in the land and a multitude of people of all ranks, accompanied the funeral car to Arlington. The coffin was placed in the sarcophagus at noon. And from that hour, an armed soldier has kept guard constantly, day and night, before that hallowed shrine.

### Fort Myer

Fort Myer was at first called Fort Whipple and it was one of the 68 forts defending the capital during the Civil War. In 1872 it was made a permanent Army post, and later, it was named Fort Myer in honor of Brigadier General Albert J. Myer, the creator of the Signal Corps of the United States Army.

Fort Myer covers an area of approximately 2 square miles, and consists of a cavalry squadron, a battalion of field artillery, and a machine gun troop. It is less than 2 miles from Washington and would be the protector of the capital in an emergency. The troops from Fort Myer and the United States Army Band are in frequent demand for various ceremonial services in Washington, as the Presidential escort and as escorts to military funerals in Washington and Arlington Cemetery.

The first airplanes owned by the United States Government were demonstrated at Fort Myer, and the Wright brothers did much of their first work here.

### Navy and Marine Memorial

This is a striking monument on the Potomac bank of the Mount Vernon Memorial Highway, near the bridge over the Boundary Channel. It represents a flock of gulls flying low over the crest of a dashing wave. It is an appropriate memorial to the heroic men who have lost their lives in service on the sea.

### The Pentagon

The Pentagon is the world's largest office building. It covers 34 acres of ground. The Capitol, immense as it is, would fill only one of its five sections.

The Pentagon was built during a wartime emergency. Twenty-four thousand workers in the War Department had filled every nook and cranny in the capital; yet more employees were needed to attend to the business of managing the affairs of an Army of more than 8,000,000 men and women in all parts of the globe. Washington streets as well as buildings were overcrowded; therefore, the Pentagon was built across the Potomac River, on the Virginia side, on land—for the most part—already owned by the Federal Government.

This unusual building was planned and built in 16 months; under ordinary conditions it would have taken four years. To accomplish this, an army of workmen was required; at one time, 15,000 were working on the job, day and night. At the same time, new roads had to be constructed to give access to the building. Thirty miles of new highways appeared as by magic, with clover leaf intersections, overpasses—2 of them—and double overpasses; and there are even some places where three highways cross one above the other. Five roads lead to the building, and a paved parking space of 46 acres was provided for the thousands of automobiles.

The pentagonal design was used with the idea of providing the greatest utility, economy of space, and a saving of walking time. The building rests upon 41,492 concrete piles, which would stretch 200 miles if they were laid end to end. The structure consists of five concentric pentagons, one placed inside the other, made of concrete reinforced with steel; only the outer perimeter is faced with limestone.

There are five floors in the Pentagon and each floor is decorated in a different color: the first floor is in brown; the second in green; the third in red; the fourth in gray; and the fifth is in blue. Stairways, escalators, and ramps lead to the different floors; the ramps are like tunnels sloping upward. There are 17½ miles of the corridors, more than 6,000,000 feet of floor area, and the perimeter of the building is one mile. Approximately 700 janitors and cleaners are needed to keep the place in apple-pie order for the 32,000 workers.

A three-lane bus terminal leads under the concourse which is on the ground floor and is reached by a stairway of one flight. The concourse, 680 feet long and 150 feet in width, is supported by many gay, orange-red pillars.

The Pentagon has been called a monument to the ability and power of the American people to meet an emergency successfully.

### Washington National Airport

When this airport was opened June 16, 1941, it was pronounced the best equipped commercial airport not only in the nation but in the world.

Early in aviation history, Washington became one of the busiest air travel centers in the country. The Washington-Hoover Airport, poorly situated, was soon outgrown and inadequate. Then President Franklin Delano Roosevelt dreamed of a horrible accident at the tiny airport. He demanded that the capital city have a new airfield.

A suitable location containing all the numerous requirements for a modern, model airport was hard to find. In fact, the matter had "been under consideration" for more than 12 years. But this was a rush order from the Chief Executive himself, so there was no more time wasted. Eighteen government agencies immediately went to work to find the proper site.

The place chosen was Gravelly Point, Virginia, across the Potomac River and just 3½ miles from the business center of Washington. Although there were only 304 acres of land in this marshy stretch along the river-side, the resourceful engineers pumped out the water and dredged the mud from the river bed to fill in the swamp; and thus they made 425 extra acres of land, giving the new airfield a total of 729 acres. Less than six years later, that field had to be enlarged. Many more acres—hundreds more—are needed.

The administration building is modern and attractive. It serves not alone as a terminal for air traffic, but as a place of entertainment for thousands of Washington visitors. A long promenade half encircles the building and a spacious dining room with broad, high windows on two sides, and an open terrace overlooking the field, add to the pleasure and comfort of the guests.

The control tower is of tinted glass to prevent sun glare, and long windshield wipers keep the windows free of snow or rain. An approach board automatically records the location of all outgoing and incoming planes. The loading docks have tiny, saucer-like turntables for the front wheel, to aid in turning the plane when it is being loaded or unloaded.

In a penthouse on the roof of the airport building is a government weather station where meteorologists make observations to detect the direction and velocity of wind currents. They release small balloons carrying radiosondes for upper air observation and also receive the radiosonde signals. The results of these observations are sent to the office of Washington's weather forecaster downstairs in the airport building, and also to every weather bureau in the country.

All modes of transportation can be seen at the airport; planes, large and small; steamboats, sailboats, motorboats, water craft of all sorts on the Potomac; automobiles on the adjacent highway; and trains on the railroads just beyond. And at night, with Washington in the distance all agleam with lights, it is a fascinating scene.

### Alexandria

Just six miles from Washington, along the Mount Vernon Memorial Highway, it is possible to find oneself in an atmosphere typical of the "Old South." Here are stately houses of faded, time-tinted brick, built out to the street; short flights of steps with elegant wrought iron railings lead from the brick pavement to the lovely arched doorways, topped by fan-shaped transoms. Behind these houses are fragrant, old-fashioned gardens snugly surrounded by tall hedges.

This is Alexandria, Virginia, George Washington's home town. It is a scant 10 miles from Mount Vernon, and it was here that Washington attended the Masonic Lodge, deposited his money in the bank, and went to Christ Church where his name plate is still on his pew.

Alexandria was founded long ago. In 1679, Peter Howsing received a grant of land—6,000 acres—on "the freshes of the Potomac," from Governor Berkeley. One year later, Captain John Alexander bought the grant for 6,000 pounds of tobacco. About 50 years after this purchase, in 1731, some Scottish merchants built a large tobacco warehouse near the harbor on Hunting Creek. They erected their houses close by and called the little village Bellhaven. It was incorporated under the name of Alexandria in 1749.

George Washington, then an ambitious young lad of 17, helped the surveyor lay out the streets.

Alexandria grew rapidly and was soon a busy tobacco-shipping port. Many fine houses were built by people whose names became prominent in our country's history. The Ramsay house, built in 1748, has been the scene of many historic events. *The Alexandrian Gazette,* the oldest daily newspaper in the United States has been in continuous circulation since it was founded in 1784, and is still published every day except Sunday. On a hill overlooking the city, the George Washington Masonic National Memorial, a $5,000,000 structure, is being erected by the Masons of America.

There are so many places of historic interest in and around Alexandria that a visitor could profitably spend several days roaming about the old town.

### Mount Vernon

George Washington's home was to him the best loved place in the world. Today it is America's most popular shrine.

The land is part of a grant of 5,000 acres given to George Washington's great-grandfather, John Washington, and his friend, Nicholas Spencer, by Lord Culpepper in 1674. George's father, Augustine Washington, built the first house on "Little Hunting Plantation," as it was called, in 1735, and lived there with his family until the house burned four years later.

Lawrence Washington, George's older half-brother, who was given this estate, built the present house and renamed it Mount Vernon, in honor of Admiral Vernon the British naval commander under whom he had served in the Caribbean. George Washington inherited Mount Vernon in 1754, but it was not until after his service through the next five years in the French and Indian War that he married the wealthy young widow, Martha Custis, and established his residence on the estate on the Potomac.

For almost 16 years, George and Martha Washington lived a life which was their ideal, in this beautiful home. The hundreds of slaves on the plantation carried on many and varied industries. Martha, in addition to supervising the countless household duties and the comfort of her family and guests, kept a corps of workers busy at their wheels and looms in the spinning house down the lane. Washington loved his farm, his prize livestock, and his rare trees and beautiful gardens.

The Continental Congress, the Revolutionary War, and two terms as President of the United States robbed Washington of 16 years of life in the home he adored. He lived at Mount Vernon only two years after serving two terms as President, and Martha died three years later.

Washington's nephew, Bushrod Washington, next inherited the estate. As it passed from one relative to another, the house, the grounds, and the land deteriorated, and the money vanished. The Washington family offered to sell the property to the Government and also to the State of Virginia; but neither the United States Government nor Virginia, Washington's native state, cared to buy it.

A patriotic South Carolina woman, Miss Ann Pamela Cunningham, organized the Mount Vernon Ladies' Association. Through the funds collected by this group, 475 acres of the estate, including the house, all the surrounding buildings, and the boat landing, were purchased in 1859. The restoration of the buildings and grounds has been made according to Washington's plans, and today, Mount Vernon is seen as he left it.

Mount Vernon is not a magnificent mansion, but a comfortable, roomy house, quite elegant for the time in which it was built. On the main floor are the large, central hall, the music room, the family dining room, the sitting room, the parlor, the banquet room, and the library. The second floor contains Washington's bedroom and dressing room, Nellie Custis' room, the guest room, Lafayette's room, the yellow room, and several other bedrooms. There are six additional bedrooms on the third floor.

Much of the furniture which actually belonged to the Washington family has been gradually recovered and installed in Mount Vernon. All of the pieces in Washington's room are originals. The large wing chair in this room is the one in which Mary Ball Washington nursed her baby son, George. Most of the furnishings on the first floor were there in Washington's time: the clock on the stairs, the marble-topped table, and the beautiful old rug in the banquet room that was given to Washington by King Louis XVI of France. The great key to the Bastille and a hunting horn were sent by Lafayette, and the hall lantern was a gift to Lawrence Washington from Admiral Vernon.

Mount Vernon is calm and lovely. There is no scene more full of peace and beauty than the view from the wide portico, down the grassy slope, across the quiet Potomac River, which is a mile in width at this particular point.

Universal respect has always been paid to Washington's memory. Each year thousands, not only Americans, but people from all lands, visit Mount Vernon. Each official or distinguished guest representing a foreign country makes a pilgrimage to this shrine to leave a wreath at the door of Washington's tomb as a tribute to his memory.

All the ships of the United States Navy, when passing Mount Vernon on the Potomac, pay tribute to the memory of our first President. It is one of the Navy's oldest customs and is listed among the "Honors and Ceremonies" in the United States Navy Regulations. President Theodore Roosevelt ordered the ceremony made official in 1906.

The frigate *Congress*, the first ship-of-war to reach the

old Washington Navy Yard, was the first Navy ship to observe this ceremony while passing Mount Vernon. This
occurred in May 1801, two years after Washington's death.

In August 1814, when the British fleet, then our enemies,
sailed past Mount Vernon, every ship fired a salute and
lowered its flag to half-mast in honor of General Washington.

The form of this ceremony has changed throughout the
years: the tolling bell has replaced the gun or cannon salute; and the hand salute is used instead of removing the
hat. Whether the full ceremony as given in the Navy regulations or a brief form is used depends on the size and
nature of the vessel. But from 1801 to this day, between
sunrise and sunset, flags are lowered to half-mast, all officials and crews give the hand salute, and the bells toll on
all United States ships when passing the tomb of our great
Washington.

# Index